MW00612301

Searching For Me

Scott Sullivan

Digital Blacksmiths, LLC

Copyright © 2019 Scott Sullivan

Published by Digital Blacksmiths, LLC

All rights reserved. No part of this book may be reproduced in any form or by any electronic or mechanical means, including information storage and retrieval systems, without written permission from the author.

ISBN: 978-1-950234-00-4 (Paperback Edition)
ISBN: 978-1-950234-01-1 (PDF Edition)
ISBN: 978-1-950234-02-8 (ePub Edition)

This is a work of creative non-fiction. Everything here is true, but it may not be entirely factual. At times events have been compressed or told out of time; other times two people are condensed to one. Once and awhile, they are embroidered. Sometimes for privacy, other times for a better read. And some names and identifying details have been changed to protect the privacy of individuals.

Cover Design by Digital Blacksmiths, LLC
www.SullysBrain.com

Scott Sullivan is a slave of Christ and husband to his wife, Angie. He is an artist and writer, living in the beautiful countryside of Lancaster, PA. He can be found at: SullysBrain.com

For an exclusive bonus chapter of this book, plus previews of new books and more, sign up for my occasional newsletter:

SullysBrain.com/news-searching

to Christ, for adopting me
to Angie, for loving me
to One Mom, for giving me life
to One Mom, for giving my life direction
to Christina, ditto

CONTENTS

Introduction

I've been many things. An artist, a programmer, a writer. But today, what I hold most valued is being a son. Three times over.

The first time was fleeting. Just days after being born, I was adopted into a second family to be someone else's son. It was as if just three days after being born, I was born again into this new family.

Growing up in this new family, I always knew I was adopted. For most of my life this was simply a piece of information I carried in the back of my mind, neither good nor bad. It just was something that happened to me days after being born. It simply, *was*.

Still, it tugged at me. As an introvert, I thought quite often about being accepted. Would my friends laugh at my jokes? Would my artwork be ridiculed? Was I liked? For years, knowing I had been adopted exaggerated those uncertainties for me. I was, after all, given away.

But why?

For a while, as a teen, I ignored those questions so that any thoughts of my biological family would fade like vapor, into the past. As an adult, though, I wondered more frequently about why I was given up for adoption.

Was it because my birth mom had been more interested in herself than me? Was it because of drugs? Was I taken from her? Was I, somehow, not what she wanted in a child? Was I a burden to her? Did she want to find me? Or did she hope to never see me again?

My life was changed more drastically than ever before when I became a son in a third family. I was born again, but this time, as a child of God. I put my faith in Jesus during my late twenties. As John wrote in the fourth gospel:

> *"To all who received him, namely the ones believing in the name of him, he gave to them the right to be born children of God, who were born, not from bloodlines, nor out of the will of flesh, nor out of the will of man, but from God" (John 1:12-13, personally translated from the Byzantine Greek text.)*

I was born again. Adopted into the most holy family. But I didn't fully grasp exactly what that would mean for me right away, partially because I still felt something missing: a sense of belonging.

※

It wasn't until my early forties, however, that God placed in me an inescapable urge to find my birth parents. At the end of 2017 I began that search.

As my journey to find them continued, I kept a personal memoir to record my thoughts and feelings so I could re-member them for years to come. As I did, I found something bigger than my search for my biological parents. God had been using this search to reveal a much larger picture to me. I realized I hadn't just been searching for my biological family.

I'd been searching for me.

It was as if there was a missing part of my life that I couldn't quite make out, like the details of a dream just after you wake up. Faceless people from a life long forgotten.

My biological family was a chain of paper doll cutouts. They were connected, yet un-personalized figures. Faceless. Nameless. With one figure missing from that chain: me.

I wondered if they missed me. While I was searching for them, God took me on a journey, revealing my own transgressions and brokenness, and what was missing from my own life.

I marvel at how God speaks to us and how he guides us. He is, as Isaiah called him, the Mighty God who is sovereign over all things. In my specific case, he guided me up and down the U.S. East Coast and across the Atlantic Ocean to Italy in search of my family. Through this search, he showed me repeatedly how to trust in him and how, even through suffering, he can show grace.

By God's will, that grace eventually led me to a house in Palm Beach, Florida, in July, 2018.

※

I remember taking a deep breath as I sat in my rental car parked in that driveway. The hot Florida sun beat down on me as I stepped out of the car and looked at the single-story house in front of me.

This was my birth mother's house.

As I walked towards the door, I knew what was unfolding in realtime was a major part of my life's story.

This story started as search for my biological family. It turned into an international journey that revealed God's grace.

I wrote this book to share with others my experience of God's guidance as I discovered the deep sense of belonging I had longed for my whole life. We who follow him are all adopted into the family of God, adopted by a loving Father who does all things for his glory and our salvation.

This is an adoptee's journey of faith, family, and belonging.

Book Smart

I was born. Three days later, I was adopted into my new family. There was absolutely nothing I did to merit being brought into a new family. It was only because someone loved me enough to want me to be in her life that I became a Sullivan that chilly January in 1975.

My new mom showed her love by adopting me before I was even born. This is something I have always cherished. I wasn't just brought into her life randomly. I wasn't forced on her. Before my birth, before I did anything to deserve it, she embraced me and actively made sacrifices to bring me into her family. This is something I have thought about often - that she did that for me. That I was chosen by her to be hers.

Mom had a kind of maturity that made people around her trust her right away. Perhaps it was because she was 33 when she adopted me, having had more life experience than a typical first-time mother. Perhaps it was her years as a nurse that had built up a personal confidence. Or maybe it was the other way around: her confidence pushed her to be the skilled nurse I, as her son, looked up to.

Regardless, she was someone I wanted to be like when I grew up. I wanted to be as smart as she was, and have the poise she projected.

Unfortunately, most of the time I felt I would never be as smart as my mom. I always felt I was two or three steps behind in understanding things, despite how patient she was in helping me with homework.

In addition to not having her confidence, I didn't look like her. While she had blonde, curly hair and moved her short, yet strong frame with precision, I was lanky, with straight, dark brown hair.

I didn't have my dad's physical build, either. He was older, already 36 by the time they adopted me. He was a tall, large man with thick black glasses (I still have 20/20 vision, even in my forties). He had darker hair, but his also had a curly wave to it.

Both my mom and dad had strong chins. I had such a strong overbite that took years of braces and retainers to correct. Even to this day, I wear a beard, strategically trimmed to try to pull out my smaller chin.

My mom must have known right away that I would notice the physical differences between us. So she told me the truth. In fact, she told me I was adopted so early in my life that I can't even remember when I first learned that fact. I just always knew.

My first concept of what it meant to be adopted began to form when my parents adopted another son in late 1980. My new brother, Shane, was eight months old when he became a part of our family.

I don't remember much of that time, but I have vivid images in my head of the place we went to adopt my brother. It was chaotic; there were lots of other kids there. It felt to me at the time that we were rescuing Shane from something. I had no idea what, but I had the strong sense my mom was saving him.

I wondered if this was where I had come from as a baby. Mom said no, but didn't elaborate. Still, the idea stuck with me and gave me a better idea of adoption. She had worked to bring him into our family out of love for him, before he could earn her love. It was a powerful idea.

I was excited to have a new brother. But, of course, as Shane grew older, I began to notice how his features were different from mine and from our parents. His face was more square than mine. Nordic-looking, with a strong bone structure and super-light, straight blonde hair, and dark eyes, where mine were blue. He and I were as physically different as we could be.

Even so, I loved having him as my little brother. We would play army outside, go skateboarding, or play in a field behind our house.

One week, when I was about 10, we went so far as to form a band. Actually, it was more like one day, but the six days leading up to that was me thinking about forming a band and then finally going to him with the idea. I had already designed the cassette tape package on a piece of paper and inserted it into a blank cassette case.

I was legit.

"Do you want to start a band?" I asked Shane, who was five years old at the time.

"Yeah!" he yelled with enthusiasm.

This was going to be awesome. We'd record the tape and be famous in no time.

It was a great plan except for the fact that neither of us knew how to play an instrument at the time. Our band broke up a few hours later.

Even when we were still young people tended to typecast us. I was "the book smart one," and he was "the athletic one." I don't know whether they were simply observing our natural attributes or whether my brother and I subconsciously grew into the roles we were assigned. Being the "book smart one" and all, I did find myself pondering which of those alternatives was more likely.

My perspective on so many things growing up was filtered through the lens of knowing I was adopted.

I can't imagine how hard it must be for someone to learn as a teenager or even an adult that they aren't biologically related to their parents. By telling me while I was young, my mom saved me the pain, or the shock, of having to learn that I was not her biological child.

The downside to this knowledge, of course, was that from a very young age I had a nagging sense that I didn't belong, as though I were an outsider looking in. I felt different.

For example, while my brother and other neighborhood kids were outside playing, I'd typically be up in my room drawing or reading. I loved animation and would spend hours making flip-books. I would lie on my stomach on the hardwood floor of my room, meticulously creating each small drawing, and then staple the collection together. Sometimes the subject was just a ball, bouncing all over a page. Other times, the flip book would feature a cartoon character or two doing physical comedy. Years later, when I got into photography and was given a camera, I'd advance from my flip-books to stop-motion flip-books, using up way too much film in the process.

Despite spending all that time in my room, I never did so because I felt shunned or disliked by my family. Quite the opposite. I knew my family loved me. They loved me so much that they knew I was doing fine up in my room, being creative. Yet, I felt a void in my life that I didn't quite understand and had a strong desire to fill it.

※

As we were growing up in the small suburb of Milton, a few miles south of Boston, my dad worked long hours, typically well into the evening. At the time, I figured it was simply because he was working harder to make more money. Later, I learned that was only partially true. The main reason was that he and my mom were in the process of separating. It was a slow separation, but by the time I was in fourth grade, he no longer lived in our house.

This led to a void that grew larger still over the years. The next year, I saw him only on weekends. Within two more years, his visits had become a month apart. Then, there were no visits at all.

From the moment he stopped living with us, my mom essentially raised Shane and me on her own.

Mom was a hard worker, but still devoted to her sons. After long days of being on her feet without rest as a nurse, caring for others, she would come home to care for us too.

As much as she took on responsibility back then, I ran from it. But she overlooked that and tried to encourage me instead. Even when I would wait until the last minute on my school projects, she would instantly stop everything to help.

One day, when I was in sixth grade, I asked her, "Can you help me build a model?" We were going over Greek mythology in class and we each had to do a project on the Parthenon, the temple of the Greek goddess Athena.

"I suppose. Do you want to work on it this weekend?" she asked.

"Well, actually," I sheepishly admitted, "it's sort of due sooner. I need it tomorrow."

I knew she was disappointed I had waited so long. But, without hesitation, she went right downstairs with me to the toolroom in our basement to help me get it started.

Piece by piece, we cut apart a broom handle to make the pillars. And while she was nailing them around the outer edge of a rectangular piece of wood we'd found lying around, I began modeling the statue of Athena out of Play-Doh.

Once I finished it, we spray painted the three-inch tall statue gold and allowed it to dry.

"That's amazing!" I said as I set the small gold statue in the center of the larger three-foot-long model of the temple. The air smelled of sawdust and spray paint. Our hands were covered in paint. And I was ready to get whatever rest I could before school.

Mom was always prepared like that. I wasn't. That trait, or my lack of it, was one of many ways we were different. Sometimes, I wondered if I'd more prepared to rise to the occasion, like her, if I *wasn't* adopted. If she was my biological mom. Maybe I'd be smarter, too. That small point of pain was like a minuscule pebble in my shoe, something that no one knew about but me, but always there.

I knew I was missing a sense of belonging, but I was afraid to verbalize it. I wanted everyone to think I fit in just fine, no matter how much I felt I didn't.

I grew up living this second life with my second family as if it was my first and only family. They were the only family I'd ever known, after all.

My mom made sure to spoil me with tools to spark my desire to learn.

One of my many special memories is of a Christmas day in the early '80s, when I was still in elementary school. After creeping downstairs in my pajamas that morning, I walked across the carpeted living room floor in my bare feet to the giant Christmas tree next to our fireplace. There were a few boxes set off to the side from the other presents, all the same size, each wrapped the same way.

Curious, but being careful not to wake my mom, I put two hands around one of them, intending to shake it to figure out what was in it.

It didn't budge. The box weighed a ton!

What is this?

I tried the box next to it. But that one weighed just as much! It didn't rattle. It just sat there.

When Mom finally made her way downstairs she had Shane and me follow her into the kitchen for breakfast. As the air filled with the smell of bacon and eggs, the two of us kept guessing at what Santa might have brought each of us.

"Army water guns!" my brother guessed. He and I loved playing army outside with water pistols, so much so that ours had both cracked under heavy usage. We could both use new ones.

"Bowling balls?" I guessed about the ones I'd tried to lift.

What else was that heavy?

She wouldn't give us even a hint. Finally, after breakfast, we bolted into the living room to start shredding the wrapping paper.

The first box I tore into didn't give any clues even after the paper was off. It was just another cardboard box.

Arrrgh!

Then I pulled open the lid, and gasped.

The box was stuffed with brown hardbound books. I pulled one of them out to open it up, not thinking to just look at the spine. It was one volume of a complete encyclopedia set: 29 volumes in all with a two-volume index. Together, they weighed more than I did.

For the "book smart" kid, this was a perfect gift.

I spent the rest of the day exploring those books and carrying them up to a shelf Mom had somehow cleared off in advance without me knowing. Yeah. She was smart like that. Once I lined up the full set, the wood shelf bowed ever so slightly under the weight of so much knowledge.

That collective gift, one of the best Christmas gifts I could have dreamt of, was something I treasured for a long time. I would sit up at night reading from those books - my first library.

Even after being told to go to bed, I'd shut off the lights, then lean over the foot of my bed, stretching my arm out to pull out a volume from the set - always being careful not to step on the creaky wooden floor and wake my mom. I'd then read entries in the dark, under my covers with a flashlight.

Yes, my childhood rebellious stage was fighting to read more of an encyclopedia. Yeah. That. But to me, it was knowledge. I craved understanding. I wanted to know how things worked.

※

One summer morning in 1986, I happened upon an encyclopedia entry on how an electric motor works. It showed me how a simple electric motor can be constructed by taking a copper wire and wrapping it around something else, then balancing it on a rotating axis to let it spin freely. By adding an alternating current to this coil, a magnetic current is created and will cause the electric motor to spin.

Since my dad wasn't around much anymore at this point, I figured I could do it on my own, though I was only eleven. I even had two bare wires coming out of my crude electric motor to supply the alternating current. Of course, there just so happened to be an outlet in the wall nearby, supplying plenty of alternating current.

Yes. I actually thought this was a good idea.

Also yes, I continued to think this as I walked over to the wall.

No, just because I had the intellectual curiosity to build an electric motor didn't mean I had the common sense to think my plan through. Apparently I was book smart, just not street smart.

One very loud pop later, I was instantly thankful that the wiring in the house had been designed well enough to blow the fuse and not my heart. To this day, I'm still amazed that I lived through that moment.

In addition to receiving that sudden, physical jolt, I received a very thorough lesson on the dangers and power of electricity. Despite their separation, on that occasion, Mom made sure my dad, the electrician, was there to give me the talk.

The phoenix that rose from the ashes of my electrical experimentation would change my life forever.

The Phoenix

Mom continued to feed my curious mind. While my school-mates got plastic water guns, she gave me a clear plastic model of a human being, filled with internal organs in various colors. The Visible Man, it was called. She would spend time teaching me how the circulatory, nervous, and muscular systems worked.

After the electric motor incident, she subtly guided my curiosity toward something a little safer and, especially, away from anything that had voltage.

It just so happened that by 1986, the personal computer had made its appearance in the consumer market. That summer, this 11-year-old was given a white TRS-80 Color Computer as a very early Christmas gift, to keep my attention away from electrical sockets - in hopes that I'd still be alive by the time December 25 rolled around.

Mom helped me carry an old wooden piano bench up from the basement to my bedroom. It was covered in pale green paint, chipped all over, but it was sturdy enough to serve as a table for this new computer and the small television screen attached to it. It was the perfect setup.

I'd spend hours creating and experimenting by writing computer programs. While the other kids were playing on jungle gyms, I was inside coding.

This first taste of computer programming gave me a love of technology that would last a lifetime. Eventually it led me to designing websites and writing apps.

The computer was perhaps my best friend. When you grow up with a brain fascinated by the process of categorizing and organizing things, people seem as frustratingly unpredictable as the weather. People did odd things, I recognized. Computers were logical. They made perfect sense.

Computers also were consistent. Each time you ran a program they gave a consistent result. People, not so much.

Not everything revolved around the computer, though. I wasn't allowed to become a complete recluse. Mom made sure of that.

※

Whenever I would actually go outside, it would be with my best friend, Carlito. In terms of personality, he was about as close to a clone of me as I could imagine. He was extremely smart and had an incredible imagination. Plus, his family was about as Italian as you could get. That fascinated me to no end.

In elementary school and into sixth grade, I spent quite a bit of time hanging out over at Carlito's house, not far from our house in Milton. I loved eating there since his mom would make foods with flavors I'd never tasted before. And his parents seemed to have quite a bit of money. Even though I had to take my shoes off at their door before going inside, I didn't mind because their kitchen had heated tiles. *Heated tiles.* How cool!

What was equally cool was the way his parents gave him an environment to be creative. Together, he and I constructed elaborate imaginary worlds.

During one particularly rainy spring, for example, we engrossed ourselves for a week in designing and then building a Lego truck that would transform into a helicopter. We'd spend our evenings consumed with building it, but thought nothing of crashing it apart in a momentary - yet splendid - explosion of pieces that scattered across the floor. Then we'd run outside to play.

There were woods just behind his house, beyond the dead-end street he lived on. We'd hop over the giant wooden-log guardrail at the end of the road and head down a slight embankment to the small creek that ran through that area. More often than not, the water level would be high enough to form more of a swamp than a creek. A muddy, shin-deep swamp that became a backdrop for our imaginations.

It was wonderful.

We watched *Indiana Jones* on VHS so often that our swamp became the Amazon River, prompting us to spend weeks searching for an archaeological artifact rumored to be buried in the surrounding jungle.

At the time, it didn't matter that our ancient artifact greatly resembled the pewter lid to my mom's antique mug. Though it did matter later, when it came back encrusted in mud.

One reason Carlito and I got along so well was that we didn't fit in well with most of the kids in our class. We liked odd things and had an odd sense of humor that nobody else seemed to appreciate. But as for the two of us, we got each other.

"You know what we should do?" he asked one day.

"What's that?"

"We could design cruise ships. But make them like the old ones. The classy ones."

The *Titanic* wreckage had just been discovered around that time and was at the front of our minds. How cool would that be! We'd be partners in a cruise line business.

"Oh, man, yeah." What a great idea! "You design the first one, and I'll design the sister ship. Then we can grow from there." We spent the next several weeks drawing cutaway views of massive cruise ships every chance we could, all based on *Titanic's* style. I even worked on my cruise ship sketches during class, sneaking creative moments as my teacher wrote on the chalkboard.

Those projects were too much fun. I suppose I thought we'd be doing stuff like that forever. But as time went on, Carlito started drifting a different way, perhaps beginning when he started smoking.

Come on, Carlito. What are you thinking? Smoking?

My mom had told me how bad it was to smoke. She showed me images of lungs and where they were in the body in my Visible Man model. It had pink lungs, whereas the smoking images looked more like burnt marshmallows. To me, it was inconceivable that anyone would voluntarily do that to their own body.

I tried telling that to Carlito, but he shrugged it off.

As we got older, I began to wonder if he was becoming less like me, or if he'd been like this all along and I was just now able to see it.

When he started wearing a black leather jacket with lots of zippers, I was intrigued, I'll admit. However, I also began to withdraw a little more. I allowed him to do more of the talking and became more introspective.

It was as if a glass wall only I could see had been placed between us. I found myself sharing things with him less and less, until, sometime during middle school, we finished drifting apart.

For me, the swamp still was a stage for adventures; but more frequently, those adventures were conducted in solitude. At times it was because Carlito was hanging out with some high school kids who also had black leather jackets. Other times, I just wanted to be on my own and think about stuff.

※

Looking back, I recognize that Carlito was one of the first people to get the glass wall treatment from me, which was odd, because I liked him so much. I liked his family, too, and I loved their food. When I started to notice girls, I even had a crush on his older sister, Sofia. Of course, I could never tell him that. I felt as though I was observing life instead of sharing it with him.

The glass wall didn't occupy all of my thinking, but I was tuned in to it. I wondered: Why couldn't I get rid of this barrier between me and the rest of the world? And if I had been so close to Carlito and now was focused on our differences, what about others? Had I missed something about them - or me - earlier on?

I began looking at people the way I looked at writing computer programs: analytically.

What's wrong with me that I can't see?

Why do I feel so isolated?

Why can't I just make friends like other kids?

I remember walking home from school one day at the beginning of 1988, as I was wrapping up seventh grade, and wondering again about why I felt introverted and isolated.

My way home in Milton took me across a four-lane parkway that had a wide grass median between the two sets of traffic. It was lined with two rows of trees and featured a worn path, which everyone used. It was a long walk that gave me plenty of time to think about why I was so alone.

As I walked, I could hear an awful *vft-vft-vft* sound quite clearly over the sounds of cars racing by. This distinct sound was coming from my corduroy pants rubbing together as I walked.

I couldn't stand those pants but I had no choice but to wear them. I'd actually been picked on at school for those corduroys - and the pastel shirts my mom had purchased.

I wish mom never bought these stupid pants for me, I grumbled to myself as I continued on the path home, blaming her for the ridicule I'd received. It struck me: were there other family-related things that made me feel so isolated? I thought back.

After a few years of separation, my parents' divorce was finalized in 1986. I had never seen them fight. But from that point on, my dad was absent from my life. Mom took his place at my Cub Scout events, which made me one of the few kids who didn't have a dad helping him with the Pinewood Derby, making a small model race car from a block of wood. While I loved that she helped me, having a mom at the Scout meetings was just one more of those many small things that made me feel different from others.

I had no way of knowing it at the time, but my father had taken to drinking quite heavily. Mom worked extremely hard to shield my brother and me from ever seeing this problem. So much so, that I wouldn't know about it until I was an adult.

From my 10-year-old perspective, I silently noticed more things with my family that I could blame for my lack of friends. Like having to wear corduroys.

It didn't matter that my family, in reality, had done nothing wrong. Blaming them was just easier than focusing on my own failure to make friends.

Meanwhile, my mom was always there, doing things for me, while I was oblivious to how much she truly loved me.

I hadn't understood the scale of the sacrifices she'd made to adopt me into her family, though I caught a glimpse of that when my brother was adopted. While I was blaming her for my failures and even, at times, yelling at her and calling her names, she continued to love me and protect me and shield me from things like my dad's drinking.

But I was about to be given a chance to reinvent myself, an opportunity to be reborn in a whole new setting. In the summer of 1988, my mom, brother, and I moved from Boston to rural Pennsylvania, to within a block of my grandparents in the countryside of Lancaster County.

※

It was a big change for us boys, then 13 and 8, but Mom knew that being close to her parents would mean she'd have more help raising us. With my dad not being around, she made an effort to ensure we'd have positive male role models in our lives to mentor us.

My grandfather was by far my biggest influence, but she also introduced me to a friend of hers who played chess, and went so far as to arrange for him to teach me the game during our first year in Lancaster.

Dr. H was a dentist, and I'd walk several blocks down our quiet street to his house. It was larger than ours, on a hill overlooking a large cow pasture. Walking up to his front door, you couldn't miss the in-ground pool and slide beside his house. And he introduced me to a game that would occupy my mind for years to come.

"Have you ever played chess?" he asked the first day I showed up.

"No. Is it hard?"

"I think you'll pick it up pretty quickly. But you can spend years learning the strategies."

Since that sounded like my kind of game, I settled in to learn it as best I could. Over the next several months, he taught me the nuances of chess. Towards the end of the summer, he even lent me a computerized chess board that would light up with tiny red LED lights as I moved the small plastic pieces to different squares. I'd practice playing for days with this device and then try to beat Dr. H in person the next week.

I loved activities like this, where I could dive in and learn.

The culture of rural Lancaster was a big influence during my teenage years. Mom and her parents were German, which wasn't surprising, considering Lancaster's heavily German culture. We ate lots of sauerkraut. We attended the same Lutheran church every Sunday.

They had been Lutherans their entire lives, and so, I grew up Lutheran as well. Mom had even driven from Boston to

Lancaster for a summer vacation when I was an infant, so I could be baptized in her parents' Lutheran church. She had made sure to keep God in my life, growing up.

But it wasn't until my middle years of high school in 1991 and 1992 that I began to understand a little more about God. It was then that I first took catechism, much later in life than most everyone else in our congregation, and I learned more about Christianity. I loved being in competition with the only other student in my class, who also happened to be an older catechism student. I tried hard to be the first to memorize the books of the Bible.

But at this point in my life, I was more in love with the idea of knowing *about* God than *knowing* God. I wasn't fed a full diet of scripture. It was only a veneer. I called myself a Christian, but, looking back, it was in name only. I had been in love with the challenge of learning about him. But my life and my actions, were still very un-Christian.

Later in high school, and then more so in college, I was exposed to opposing views that made me begin to question what I had believed.

For example, I was told the Bible was only written down after several generations of being verbally being passed down, like the telephone game, over decades or centuries. How could I trust that what it said was accurate, let alone true? I began to doubt that the Bible was this perfect book from God.

Years later, by my third year of college, so much doubt had eroded my already weak faith that I stopped believing altogether. Oh, I'd still go to church at Christmas when I came home. I loved the feeling of being with family, complete with the warm glow from all the candles the congregation would hold during the service. I didn't hate religion by any means. I just felt I knew more than Christians did by that point. And, of course, I felt they were wrong and I was right.

I found myself, more and more, looking at my family in the same way I had looked at Carlito. My introverted and analytical self was picking out the ways that I was different from them, and wondering why.

A Nerd at the Beach

Ever since I was a child, Mom's side of the family, including both of her parents, siblings, nephews, and nieces, had been taking an annual week-long beach trip to Stone Harbor, New Jersey. Even back when we lived in Boston, we would drive down to meet them in Stone Harbor. It was a tradition her parents had started decades ago, when my mom was a kid.

But in my head, I questioned the point of it. Why would people drive hundreds of miles in a packed car just to sit in the sun? The way I saw it, the sun was just as hot and would shine for just as long in our backyard as it did at the beach.

I had started thinking this when we still lived in Boston, before we moved. Our backyard was significantly closer and less crowded. Besides, if we wanted the ocean, Boston had one, too. On the southeastern side, we even had a cool castle on an island. *A castle!* Jersey had nothing on that. But we continued going, year after year.

Our move from Boston to Lancaster in 1988 made it easier to make the trip in a more unified way, which gave me a chance to observe all the peculiar habits my family had. I questioned the purpose of the trips, simply from a practical level.

"I don't get why we have to drive to the beach each year," I recall whining from the back seat. The car was packed with a week's worth of clothes, food, and beach chairs, leaving very little room for my brother and me.

"It's a chance to spend time with your family," Mom said.

"But Mother doesn't go to the beach," I pointed out. "She stays in the beach house all day."

"Mother" was my grandmother. Mom and her siblings had called her that since they were kids, and the name just stuck.

"She likes having everyone together," Mom replied. "And you like playing cards each evening, right?"

I sighed. There was no winning this one. And she was right about playing cards. Most nights at the beach house, we would all gather around the table as a family and play card games.

It was a loud and fun time, with occasional shouts of "Oh Shaw!" and hands slapping their cards on the table. My grandfather, you see, had renamed a popular card game so that the words we shouted were more G-rated than the original title.

As a bonus, one or two nights during our stay, we'd walk in our beach sandals a few blocks to Stone Harbor's downtown. There we would have ice cream and play miniature golf on the roof of one of the buildings.

※

As much fun as I had, I continued to focus on the differences I saw. Most often, I was asking what made my family different from me. Surely they were the odd ones, right? Then I began to speculate that I was actually the one who didn't fit, who was socially awkward and insecure and kept to myself.

I was a nerd, trying to fit in when I was fully out of my natural environment. Give me a book and a quiet spot and I'd be happy. Give me an electrical outlet and my computer and I'd be happy.

Heck, I even ran on the cross-country team as my one sport. I loved it because I was out there, running for miles. On my own. Thinking.

But throw this scrawny kid on a beach and make him walk around, trying to look cool? Forget it.

What intrigued me most of all - what I was dying to know - was how they all seemed able to have such natural conversations among themselves and even with strangers. How did they get along so well with people?

Why was I so awkward at having conversations and making social connections? The older I got, the more I wanted to understand it all.

Even at this early time in my life, the solitude of my mind had become the one place where I could retreat. I transformed the beach trips into a playground for my imagination, enjoying the worlds I created on my own.

My younger brother didn't see things as I did. Though we'd both been adopted, and from different families, he was never anything but "my brother" - never "my adopted brother." Yet we were undeniably different. And as we grew up, my bond with him seemed to parallel my journey with Carlito. My brother and I would play, but he was much more into skateboarding and physical activities than I was. I preferred puzzles and creating impossible things.

In 1986, right before my first year of middle school, I had a Polaroid camera along on one of our family beach trips. I had just seen a book on optical illusions and wanted to try my hand at it.

"Come get a picture of us!" I yelled to Mom, who was sitting on her beach chair in the sand. I had already told Shane to go stand on a wooden pier about thirty feet away.

"Can you hold the camera here and get a picture of me so it looks like I'm holding him in my hand?" I asked her.

There I stood, with my six-year old brother in the distance, my palm up and to the side, and my mom properly positioned with the camera so it looked like my brother was standing on my hand and only a foot tall. It took a few tries for her to get it lined up just right with my hand. In the meantime, I could hear Shane complaining in the distance, asking if he could get down off the pier.

"Got it!" I finally shouted to him. "Come look!"

He immediately hopped down and ran back to us, peering over my arm to see the picture as it gradually developed.

"That's cool, I guess," Shane said, sounding unimpressed. He grabbed his foam bodyboard and went back to riding waves in the ocean, and Mom went back to her chair to watch him. I stood in the hot sand, marveling at my clever photo. Even at this young age, Shane was much more social than I.

Another year, after reading an article about what lies beneath the Earth's crust, I had him help me dig a hole in the sand so I could collect some magma. The rising tide put an end to that expedition.

I also tried to include him in an archaeological adventure that was eerily similar to a trip Professor Indiana Jones had taken. I dug several small circular holes an inch or two deep in the sand near the lifeguard's rowboat, then called him over.

"Those holes in the ground are traps," I said to him. "If you step on them, they trigger darts that shoot out of the side of the boat."

"I guess." Shane didn't appear convinced.

"And they have poison on them. So we have to be careful or we die!"

"Sure. So we get past them to get to the water and play?"

"No," I explained. "We have to steal that golden skull off of the pedestal over there on the other side."

Shane squinted skeptically. "That looks like a plastic beach shovel."

"It is. But, I mean, it's a golden skull."

He had a harder time seeing it. He also didn't seem to agree that the rowboat had poison darts in it.

I decided that I would send him back to Professor Jones' university to get more supplies and funding so that I could focus more on the adventure. He looked at me with a puzzled face and walked back to our mom, aunts and uncles, who were reading paperback books while tanning over by the beach umbrella.

My mom took him down to the water to play in the waves.

I went back to risking my life to get the golden skull.

※

A few years later, in 1992, the subject of universities and beaches resurfaced during my junior year of high school. Only this time the location wasn't New Jersey. It was Florida. And the university wasn't a fictitious one belonging to Indiana Jones, but rather Embry-Riddle Aeronautical University in Daytona Beach.

Most kids want to be an astronaut at one point in their life. So did I. But most kids grow out of that phase and move on. I, instead, went to Space Camp. Twice. Yeah. Once in elementary school, and then again in middle school.

I also read that most space shuttle pilots were aerospace engineers. So naturally, I wanted to be a rocket scientist when I was in high school. Because, why not?

As an outsider looking in, I had begun to play deductive games with myself. I'd watch the world through my imaginary glass wall, as though life was a movie and I was Sherlock Holmes. That way I could scrutinize my surroundings and infer things about people from the smallest clues.

The more I did this, the more I found myself observing conversations rather than joining them. When I did take part in a conversation, it was too often at a level that was a few steps too far ahead to be understood. By my first year of high school, I'd stopped caring to even explain my jokes. It wasn't worth it.

Silence became a defense mechanism. I wouldn't get odd stares if I just kept my comments to myself, especially when I knew the recipient wouldn't understand. I withdrew more. For the life of me, I just couldn't figure out how to relate to my classmates. Though I tried to hide it, my isolation and loneliness continued to grow.

One way that I was different from other kids was the way I'd procrastinate about doing homework. Some classmates put if off simply because they hated homework. I did it because I knew I could complete it during the few minutes prior to class starting. In computer class, I was writing complex programs that graphically drew a mathematically generated cosine-wave screen saver while the rest of the class was still trying to get their program to add two numbers together.

In early 1992, during my junior year of high school, my different nature came to light again as I was looking into colleges. One of the few friends I did have, Mike, asked which ones I was applying to.

"I'm going for Penn State and also applying to HACC and one other," he said. He really wanted to go to the state school for history or political science, but, like most students, he had backups, just in case.

"I'm sending my application to Riddle," I replied, referring to Embry-Riddle, the top aerospace engineering school in the country.

"Anywhere else?" he asked. "What if you don't get in?"

I shrugged. "I really just want to go to Riddle. Maybe I'll send one to Penn State. But I doubt it."

In reality, I downplayed the singularity of that choice to Mike that day. But a few months later, when it came time to send in my applications, Embry-Riddle was the only application I sent in, knowing that by the time I heard back, if I didn't get accepted, it would be too late to apply to another school. I licked the envelope to the application and dropped it in the mailbox.

This is just a formality, I thought. *I'll be accepted.*

Fortunately for me, I was accepted. I would be attending the top aerospace school in the country.

Into the Deep

When I began attending Embry-Riddle in the fall of 1993, I decided that I no longer wanted to be the introverted outcast afraid of being rejected that I had been in elementary school. Nor did I want to be the introverted outcast afraid of rejection that I'd been in high school.

Simply put, I didn't want to be that nerd on the beach. I was going to make friends with the cool students this time. I was going to shatter that glass wall.

This was the major leagues.

This was college.

And what a college it was. Being in Daytona, there were palm trees all across the campus, and the quad we crossed between dorms was a mix of sand and thick, hard Florida grass. It was also a dream for me. The university was located, literally, at the airport, since it also was a flight school. We had planes taking off and landing constantly.

It was also only an hour north of Kennedy Space Center. During my first October there, a friend invited me to go with him to see a shuttle launch.

Not long after came a spectacular night launch I got to see from farther away.

"Scott, there's a shuttle launch just before dawn tomorrow morning," another student told me. "Want to meet up to watch it?"

"That's a pretty far drive," I told him. "And I don't have a car."

"But STS-61 is a night launch. You can see it from campus."

"What? No way!"

I was pumped. Sure enough, just before 4:30 in the morning, on December 2, a bunch of us went out into the quad and looked south. It took just a few minutes of waiting to see it: a giant flame rising up from the horizon, like a yellow blowtorch climbing into the night sky.

Seeing actual shuttle launches so frequently motivated me tremendously to study, which was good because the classes could be intense. Many focused on developing the proper analytical skills to ensure our designs would fit within extremely narrow tolerances.

In addition to studying my classwork, I would study my classmates. Rarely was I ever "in the moment." I would constantly find myself channeling two parallel streams of thought at once.

The first would be the one that was talking to them, answering questions, and the like. The second train of thought was observing them, analyzing them, and attempting to categorize them.

I found myself doing this even more, most regrettably, with my roommate. I'd met him on my first day at the college, in the fall of 1993. When I first walked into the small two-person dorm room, it was completely empty except for the twin beds, desks, and bureaus. So I began unpacking my things on the left side of the room. After about an hour, I heard a knock.

Standing at the door was another student, with backpack and suitcase.

"Hi, I'm Brian," he said to me with a smile. His skin was smooth and extremely pale.

I wondered how often, if ever, he went outside. *Probably spent more time at the computer than even me*, I thought. He had an older-style pair of glasses that looked like they were a pretty heavy prescription.

I instantly jumped to the conclusion that I was rooming with a nerd with very few friends - like I was in high school. Looking back, I hate that I categorized him like that.

"Hey," I replied. I was still trying to figure out how to take him. We talked a bit longer, but I could tell he was more introverted than I was. As we each continued unpacking for our first semester, we talked about where we were from and our respective degrees.

"I'm going for aerospace engineering," I told him. "How about you?"

"Physics."

As I got to know him in those first few weeks, I typecast him as everything I was in high school and everything I didn't want to be in college. Over the weeks and months, our conversations became more sporadic, and I'd spend more time with other aerospace engineers down the hall. When we were in our room at the same time, we lived in our own worlds, coexisting but not interacting.

I began to dislike him. Or was I disliking me? *Was I hiding my insecurity with an outward arrogance?*

I quickly dismissed those thoughts. It was much easier to convince myself that it was his fault. As the first semester continued, I saw him more and more as the high school version of me that I didn't like. I wanted badly to be something I was not: the cool extrovert. Brian was too introverted; I needed to break my own introverted mold and find cool friends. Extroverted friends, the kind who were the hit of the party.

※

Embry-Riddle was known for turning out some of the top commercial pilots in the country. The pilots had a reputation for partying a bit more than the engineers.

Really, though, that wasn't hard. When engineering students partied, it was usually a bunch of nerds collecting red plastic beer cups and, instead of chugging from them like normal college kids, using them to build a replica of a Saturn 5 rocket. I hated to admit I was in the engineering party group. I desperately wanted to be in the pilot circle.

I'm not sure how I'd missed it in those first few weeks, but one evening towards the end of September 1993, I was hanging out at a fellow engineering student's dorm room when I noticed an odd light coming from the room across the hall. It was mostly dark in the room, and I couldn't see anyone in there.

Curious, I walked over and knocked on the open door.

"Come on in," he said a voice with a distinct Southern accent.

I slowly walked inside and immediately noticed the source of the odd lighting. The curtain was closed, and the occupants had strung white Christmas lights along the window and bunk beds. So far, I was intrigued.

To the right, along the wall and hidden from the hallway, I could now see the guy with the accent. That is to say, I could see his back. He was sitting at his desk, on which sat a giant computer monitor displaying the most advanced flight simulator I'd ever seen. He also didn't have a mouse: instead, there was an airplane yoke attached to the computer somehow.

This guy was serious about flying.

"Hey, I'm Scott," I said to his back.

He turned around and introduced himself with a super friendly tone. "Hey, I'm Jonathan. How ya doin'?"

"I'm good. Saw your room from across the hall. Pretty sweet."

"Thanks. Helps me practice for night flights. You want a drink?"

Since I did, I stayed and we talked. Eventually, his roommate returned: a fellow pilot-to-be named Sam, whose parents had moved from Cuba to Florida a few years ago. He was dressed in a short sleeved, button down linen shirt and khaki pants. Classy.

"Hey," he said, introducing himself. His Cuban accent was super thick and he played that up.

"Scott," Jonathan said, "he doesn't like to let many people know, but he's one of Fidel's nephews."

Sam nodded his head. "It's where I got most of my money."

For a short while, I believed them both until they both broke into laughter. I had been had. While Sam did have quite a bit of money, he was in no way related to the Cuban dictator.

He was, I found out, a star baseball player on his high school team. Most of the baseball items I had seen in the room were his. He said his parents moved to Florida years ago and had done very well - enough to send him to Embry-Riddle.

As he said this, I figured they both had money, from the way they dressed and the items in their room. As the semester continued, I ended up hanging out there more and more.

They were cool and sophisticated – upper classmen who knew how to party... without stacking their cups like a rocket. Their cups were filled with soda. Mixed with rum. As, I thought, they should be.

For the first time in my life, and with their help, I learned to party. And what better place to do it than in Daytona Beach.

There were other things I loved about that group, such as the short drives we'd take down to the beach and bars after classes, several of us piled in the back of a pickup truck. Daytona's beach is one of the finest I've seen. You really are allowed to drive on it, and the sand is a soft, fine grain that slopes gently down to the water.

I loved it there.

At that time, there was a sandbar a short distance out in the water. During high tide, once we swam out far enough, the sandbar allowed us to stand shoulder-deep in the warm Florida water. It was relaxing to make this routine trek of going out to the sandbar each evening that semester to enjoy the quiet beach and tranquil waves.

Out there, we'd have profound conversations about how to solve the world's problems. I'll admit, I noticed this group often got their facts wrong, but I bit my tongue and said nothing. I deeply wanted to be accepted and enjoy that sense of belonging with them.

It was during those conversations, out in the ocean, that I found myself drifting, literally and figuratively. Questions were brought up about my faith that I couldn't answer.

Sure, I had memorized the order of the books of the Bible. I had learned what communion meant when we took part in the Lord's Supper. But I had not been fed a full diet of the word of God. I didn't understand the unifying thread of the Messiah that seems woven through every page of scripture.

Having learned that God is love, and that God loves us, was great. But when that is as deep as it went, when the harder questions came, I had no answer.

How can you believe a book that says the universe was created in seven days when science shows it is billions of years old?

Couldn't Jesus have faked his death?

Don't you find it ironic that the closer you get to the Middle East, the more violent it gets?

I simply had no response for these, nor the many more questions that followed.

So floating silently under the stars on those warm nights, my faith slowly drifted away from me. For awhile, I began calling myself agnostic, trying to hold onto to something of a spiritual foundation. Then even that was too much. I saw only the science and logic of the physical world and rebelled against a god that would kill his own son. Fully rejecting God, the idea of atheism had pulled me in.

I began drifting in those warm, inviting waters of unbelief, and continued drifting for the next several years of my life.

But even as I had these conversations with my pilot friends, something just wasn't quite right. I kept trying all semester - trying to be like guys who went downtown and partied and hung out in the ocean having late-night chats. I had fun with them, but it didn't feel natural.

I still wasn't truly living "in the moment." I was still fearful of saying something embarrassing. And I was still the introverted analyzer. So I observed them, hoping that eventually I would feel that I truly belonged. That tiny stone remained in my shoe.

The next semester I was talking to some engineering friends about this ritual and one particular chat we'd had at the sandbar. As I related the story, they looked at me oddly. At first, I assumed they were reacting to the odd comments of the pilots and expected them to start making fun of them. Then my stomach slowly filled with butterflies. It wasn't what I was talking about that provoked that look. It was *where* I was talking about. One engineer told me that nighttime, just off the sandbar, is when and where sharks feed.

I'd been trying so hard to be liked by the cool crowd that I had gone swimming in the same waters as sharks. While the chances were pretty slim of something terrible happening, that was a little too close for comfort for me. I never joined them at the sandbar again.

But what a story I'd have for years to come. I had been swimming with the sharks and lived to tell the tale. How often does that happen?

A Slow Sunrise

They say that chess is one of those games that's easy enough for a kid to learn, yet can take years to master. I learned that back with Dr. H., and it seemed to hold true through college and beyond.

I loved the depth that chess offers. I still do. There's an endless potential to learn more. It's the same reason I keep so many unread books in my study - that potential for knowledge. Whether or not I finish all those books doesn't matter. I want to surround myself with an endless queue of things to learn. Knowledge that I may someday conquer.

Conquer is the best word I can think of for this. When I go to learn something, I do it with the attitude that I must either master it or admit that it has mastered me.

For example, as a kid I learned countless magic tricks. The highly technical nature of executing complex card and coin "moves" requires an inordinate amount of dexterity and dedication. I found I had a natural skill and spent hours each evening practicing. It was a perfect hobby for someone as introverted and analytical as myself.

I dropped magic for years, but then in college, I discovered that I could do card tricks at private parties and get paid for it. It was an awesome way to make some spending money.

On weekends around campus, I found I got an increasing number of these magic jobs, and eventually I was able to pay for my rent, car, and food with money earned as a magician.

After college, in 1997, I thought about entertaining as a magician full time for a while before taking a permanent job. This was the time to try it. I was only 22 and hadn't begun looking for a job yet, nor did I have a mortgage or a family to support. So I jumped in with both feet - mostly, I think, to prove to myself that I could do it. But also, after years of studying math and science, there was a large part of me that was craving to get back into something artistic.

I moved back to central Pennsylvania after Embry-Riddle and met another magician who had been working full time, securing much of his work through an agent. He introduced me to that agent, and I began doing magic for bigger events. Soon, I was performing at several hotels and nightclubs in the Poconos, a resort area in northeast Pennsylvania.

Though I had never planned on this while in college, by the time I was 23, I was a full-time professional magician. Performing gave this introvert a crutch to help him talk to girls. One girl in particular was an artist who happened to work at the same resort where I was entertaining as a magician. I had noticed her a few times when we happened to be booked simultaneously. She had dark blonde hair and a confidence about her that drew me to her. On a Friday night in 1997, a mutual friend invited her out to see us perform.

Her name was Angie.

"It's a fun show," Ian told her. "One of us juggles, I do big illusions, and Scott does sideshow magic. It's a great combination. Come on out."

"It's been a while since I stayed for one of the shows," she answered. "Sure. That sounds fun."

That particular resort had been a hit destination in the '70s. Ironically, when I mentioned to my mom that I was working there as a magician, she told me it was where she and my dad had gone for their honeymoon. *Well, that's pretty cool,* I thought. *What a small world.* She told me how amazing and popular the resort had been when they went there.

By the late '90s, though, its age was showing, as were the cigarette-smoke stains on the yellow tiled ceiling, which had presumably once been white. While these resorts were no longer in their prime, they still drew a large number of guests, and this was a fun place for me to perform. I met many other magicians, comedians, and jugglers during this time.

The bands would play music for a good part of the evening, then take a break while we entertained. The resort would extend the thrust stage out over the dance floor for us. Then, we'd each do our routine. When it was my turn in the lineup, I'd make my way out with lit torches. I breathed fire, escaped from a straitjacket, and did card tricks. I wrapped up my portion of the show by pounding a nail into my nose.

All of this was about as far away as I could get from an engineering job, but I got incredible gratification from the artistic outlet it gave me. Intrigued, Angie decided to stay after the show to chat.

She carried herself differently than most of the young women I had been used to, back in college. She was different; more sophisticated. She was dressed professionally, yet artistically, since she had just come from drawing at the resort.

I'd found I could be someone else on the performance stage. I could be an extroverted, joking, cool guy. But once I walked off the stage, I was right back to my introverted self.

This night was different. As we sat at a table talking that evening, I found myself connecting with Angie in a way I hadn't experienced with anyone in years. Even in those first few hours, I began to feel like I could trust her with anything.

At some point, I realized that, for once, I wasn't analyzing her. I didn't have a parallel thought process pulling myself out of the moment to analyze and take mental notes of what was going on. Instead, I was actually just in the moment with her. It was incredible.

I knew as I talked with Angie that she got me. As an artist, she experienced the same fear of rejection I had. She'd had friends growing up that she loved to spend time with, whose behavior she often disagreed with—much the way I had with Carlito.

From time to time, as we got to know one another, I'd wonder what was different about Angie that allowed us to get along so well. Why were we so easily forming a close bond?

At the time, I never really pursued that question, because I was so happy at the moment to feel that bond with her. I could wait to figure out why we connected the way we did. I didn't want to analyze. I just wanted to enjoy my time with her. We had so many similarities; the same sense of humor, the same drive to push ourselves hard.

But she also believed in God. I didn't.

Since losing my faith during those nights in college out at the sandbar, I had left my Lutheran upbringing far behind.

As a magician, I understood psychology and deception. I could easily see how one carpenter from 2,000 years ago could deceive so many and start a new religion. Now add a small group of twelve "roadies" who called themselves disciples. It was obvious to me that those twelve could help pull off incredible magic tricks and tell stories that would make Jesus seem larger than life. Even godlike.

At the time, I was thinking: *How could someone in today's world believe in that nonsense?* It was beyond me how someone could believe in an invisible god. Normally, I looked down at believers for being uneducated and falling for psychological manipulation.

But I couldn't categorize Angie like that. She was very much like me, and to look down on her would be almost like looking down at myself.

I knew that many people who professed belief in God were really just in it for themselves. Rather than living a life of faithful service, they wanted nothing more than a "get out of jail" card to avoid going to hell. I was even told this by some Christians trying to convince me to believe that Jesus was God.

"If he isn't God, then you haven't wasted that much energy in believing in him," they'd tell me. "But if he is God, by believing you'll have won the eternity lottery." Or something along that line.

Angie wasn't like that, though. The longer we dated, the more I saw how genuine her faith in Jesus was. She didn't love people just to gain "St. Peter Points" to cash in at the gates. She loved people because, well, she loved people. And people loved her back. Angie had something I hadn't seen in many people before: true love for others. And others accepted her in the same way.

In this way, she was the exact opposite of me: with Angie, there was no glass wall keeping people out. She could bond with others easily. I craved this, and seeing it in her every day heightened my desire to learn the secret to building an unbreakable bond with others, like the one I now had with her.

When I asked what made her like this, she told me that it was all driven by her love for God. I saw it wasn't an act. It was real. Even as a full-blown atheist for several years now, my curiosity was piqued. Love for God?

One reason I had decided I didn't believe in Christianity was what I saw as the numerous contradictions in the Bible. There were just too many of them, I thought.

Around 1999, shortly after meeting Angie, I had a conversation that would challenge that view. Once a week, I would eat dinner with a musician at the resort. Pete was from England but had been living in Manhattan and drove out to the resorts each weekend to play a Stick, a unique electric guitar that was missing the body of the instrument, which made it look like just a very long neck. Every week, with his long, black hair draped over his tuxedo, he would stroll around the room playing for patrons, talking as he played.

With his British accent, Pete could have talked about doing his taxes and people would have hung on every word. He was cool like that. And like Angie, he was a believer and incredibly well-studied in the Bible.

"Pete," I said to him over dinner one night, "you know the celebration as Jesus entered Jerusalem? One of the stories has him entering Jerusalem with a donkey. Another says a donkey and a colt. If they couldn't even get that straight, what else did they make up?"

"Would it be true if I said that you ate dinner with me?" he asked.

I nodded in agreement. He continued.

"Would it be true if I told someone I ate dinner with you and Ian?"

Catching on to where he was going, I turned and looked at Ian, sitting across from us. I paused before saying yes.

"Neither is a contradiction of the other," he explained. "Just a level of amount of detail that was recorded in the account."

This jolted me the way the electric motor I had built as a kid jolted me when I stuck the wires into the wall. Except there was no fuse this time. It was my mind that short-circuited.

There was no denying it; I had to agree with him. He was right. This explanation was the first crack in my ironclad view of the Bible being a book filled with errors. Pete and his logical, calm, polite explanation, helped show me that the error was not in the text, but rather in my preconceived notions about it.

As 1999 marched on, I discovered more examples like this. My previous view of the Bible was showing broader cracks. I was no longer seeing a book to disprove. I was starting to see God. But my turn to faith unfolded slowly, without a sense of the deep connectedness I would later experience.

Many - heck, most - Christians I have met could tell me the day they first believed. They have explained, often with enthusiasm, how they felt that day, and could tell me all about that moment. I never had that moment, though.

Instead, I had a full year of much smaller steps, filled with Angie showing me the emotional side of God's love and Pete patiently teaching me the logical side of God's word. In place of a single moment when I began to believe, God allowed me to soak it in over the year, like a warm and colorful sunrise.

I recall a memorable sunrise almost two decades later, in 2017, when I traveled to Israel and stayed at a hotel on the shores of the Sea of Galilee, the very shore where Jesus once walked. Each morning before dawn I went to sit on the rocky beach to watch the sun come up over the waters and paint magical colors in the sky.

And the year 1999 was, spiritually, like that sunrise - beginning in darkness with a few twinkles of light, and alone and with a dark outlook. Pete and Angie's love for me, like that Galilean dawn, had a profound effect on me.

As these progressive revelations presented themselves, it was like seeing that first soft glow of purple in the early morning. Then, without actually noticing the moment when it happens, the first hints of color creep into the lower edges of the sky. There are glimmers of light.

Before 1999, words in the Bible had been just black and white letters to me. Now, they were beginning to show depth and insight. There was a wisdom in these writings that became as clear to me as the oranges that overtake the deep blues of a predawn morning. I was starting to see the full spectrum of the Bible's meaning.

As the sun rose higher, creeping above the mountains on the other side of the Sea of Galilee, I felt it warm my heart. Just as the Bible's words did when they illuminated the richness of God's grace and love for us, his creation. Eventually, God's light was permeating my entire being, even more than the burning brightness of the morning sun. His love sank deep into my soul.

It was a beautiful journey.

Over the next four years, Angie and I grew closer. I grew to love her in a way I had never felt before. It was a love that knew no bounds. I could trust her with anything. And I especially loved that I could just be me with her, in the moment, without analyzing. When I was with her, I felt free and at ease.

In October 2004, she and I were married in a small ceremony at my grandfather's house, near where I grew up, with our closest family members present. It was an incredible moment, having just our immediate family there.

Angie and I lived about an hour from my mom, so I still saw her frequently, and we talked on the phone regularly.

But it was special to see her and Dad at the same time, which had hardly happened at all after their divorce. My dad had moved from Boston to Fort Meyers, Florida, a few years earlier. I had rarely seen him even when he lived in Boston, but with his move to Florida, there were no visits at all. My wedding was the first time I had seen him face to face in years.

It was a great celebration and a potent reminder to me of the importance of family as I stood there with my family and Angie's.

※

Spiritually, I felt refreshed. I also found a new a path to grow artistically. As we entered the new millennium, and I entered my thirties, I found my career as a magician shifting. After about a decade of performing at countless resorts as a master sleight-of-hand artist—and winning awards among my peers - I gave it up. I needed new subjects to master.

Graphic design was a skill I'd had to learn to market my skills as an entertainer effectively. I'd always been an artist. For the most part, it was a hobby that I enjoyed and was pretty good at. But I had to go from "pretty good" to top of my game to create the quality of business cards, advertisements, and websites I needed to book myself as an entertainer. So I studied graphic design to improve my artistic skills.

By the mid 2000s, I became so good at it that I began free-lancing as a motion graphics artist. I even started my own company to do graphics and animations for entertainers.

My compulsion to master any skill I learned—like diving into chess, magic, and engineering - kicked in again. Now, I wanted to create the best designs possible, so I'd spend countless hours in the evenings studying design on my own.

This continued until, in 2008, I was offered a position as a full-time motion graphics artist and animator for a video production and design company in Harrisburg, one of the largest in central Pennsylvania.

Prior to this, Angie and I had lived near Pottsville, to the northeast, which allowed us to be close to Angie's family as well as the Poconos. But when I took the job in the state capital, we looked for houses within a half-hour drive from my job.

We found a beautiful colonial house in rural Lancaster County, just miles from the house I had moved to with my mom and brother back in 1988. I was back in my old stomping ground.

My mom still lived in that house, so I was able to drive over there more often and spend more time with her, which was an added benefit.

The artistic side of me thrived when I entered graphic design, which allowed me to express myself and communicate ideas in ways I never could as a magician. Creating something from nothing is magical in itself.

As I grew as an artist, the work also allowed me to dive deeper spiritually. If ever there was a relationship that I craved, this was it. I had never imagined I would be pouring myself into building a relationship with God like this. I hoped this would be the catalyst for eliminating my feeling of isolation and would help put to rest forever my fear of being alone.

So I treated the Bible like a college course. I researched and studied it every moment that I could. When I learned that the original writings of the New Testament were in Greek, I found a Greek professor to tutor me. For four years, beginning in 2014, I studied biblical Greek so I could not only read it but understand its nuances and depth.

One of my favorite studies happened as I worked on my own translation of John's gospel from the Byzantine Textform, a name given to a collection of Greek manuscripts of the New Testament. I was looking into John's description of how Christ (called The Word here) dwelt among us. It is a phrase with incredible depth.

The Greek word that we translate in most Bible translations as "dwelt" has a rich background. Etymologically, it is closer to "pitched his tent" or "tabernacled."

> *"And the Word was made flesh and pitched his tent among us - and we perceived the glory of him, such glory as the only, one of a kind, Son from the Father - full of grace and truth." (John 1:14, personally translated from the Byzantine Greek Text)*

To better understand the depth of this verse, it is good to understand the two "realms" used in scripture. One is God's heavenly realm; the other, the realm of humanity. Imagine them as two circles that intersect only rarely. One of those times is described in the first pages of scripture, when God walks among his people in the Garden of Eden. When God banishes Adam and Eve from the garden, the circles go from being almost fully overlapping to being almost fully separate.

Generations later, God instructed the Hebrew people to build a holy area to allow for priests to approach God. This was a very specifically designed tent, called a tabernacle, and in it was the tiny spot where those two circles overlapped. Only the most holy priests could enter the innermost chambers of this tabernacle and, even then, only after cleansing themselves spiritually. This enabled the chosen priest to be, essentially, in the presence of God and heaven. This tabernacle eventually evolved into the more permanent Temple in Jerusalem.

So when John describes how Jesus came to earth to dwell with us, it is with great significance that he chose to describe Jesus as having "tabernacled" among us. John is saying that God himself is dwelling here on Earth in Jesus. Jesus is the temple. It is a strong, deep, and very intentional description that weaves together the entire Bible.

It is depth like this that drew me into God's story. There's a reason Jesus refers to the idea of his disciples being "fishers of men." The story snares you in a net and pulls you along. Like chess, it's a story simple enough for a child to understand, yet deep enough to spend a lifetime in study.

The Bible became more beautiful the more I studied it, both in Greek and English. I wanted to study Hebrew, to be able to explore the Old Testament better, but that one would wait for now. But it was all beautiful. Far from the book of contradictions I initially thought it was, I could now see how this collection of scriptures from various points in time was the most consistent and perfect story ever written.

This time, it wasn't surface-level knowledge, as it had been for me in high school. I was coming to a much deeper understanding. Each week, we'd attend a service at a local Lutheran church. I'd spend evenings studying scripture and translating the New Testament from the original Greek. And I kept seeing even more beauty in God's story.

※

For me, the most beautiful part of the story is God's choice of adoption to bring us into his fold. We are born into sin, he tells us. But he does the work of changing us and giving us a new heart, so that we can be reborn and be adopted into his family.

In the first chapter of Paul's letter to the Ephesians, God teaches us how he set everything up before the creation of the world, so that he could adopt us, out of love. The effort he made to adopt us is amazing. It wasn't an afterthought; it was the main thought.

Paul's letter to the Galatians expands on this, saying in the fourth chapter that when God's timeframe was ready, he sent Jesus Christ for the purpose of dying in our place so that God could adopt us into his family. Not only did God choose us, but he paid the full price for us so that we could be with him.

When I was just days old, my mom adopted me into her family. It was not because I had done well on a test or because I had saved up enough money to earn a ticket to be adopted. It was because she loved a child, even before that child had been born. In the same way God had loved me before I'd even acknowledged his existence. God had used that year with Angie and Pete to bring a beautiful sunrise to my soul, to warm my heart, and to show me the colorful depth of the Bible.

Just as I was adopted, God adopts us.

I loved that, for so many reasons! If God could embrace us that way, then perhaps, as an adopted child of God, I could find that sense of belonging I had been missing my whole life. I waited for that bond to materialize. For a short time, this sunrise had warmed my heart. I basked in this new warmth and brilliance. I saw no sunset in my future.

An Approaching Sunset

The yearlong spiritual sunrise as I turned 30 gave me a dedication I never could have imagined. God had revealed himself to me, a dedicated atheist, turning me into a slave of Christ, as even Paul preferred to call himself. The best part was thinking that this could be the catalyst to change the course of my life.

But somehow it was having the opposite effect. My analytical nature kicked in, and after a few years, I began to overthink things.

By my late thirties, that sunrise was turning into a sunset. As much as I wanted to teach others about God's love, I felt slightly cursed. I seemed to see only flaws - in myself and in other people. I allowed myself to think that most other Christians held views that were incorrect and ran against the Bible's teaching. I wrongly convinced myself that the number of Christians who *got it* was even smaller than I'd originally thought, and not growing. It was a dangerous perspective, believing that other Christians were flat-out wrong when their views were simply different from my own.

I was rejecting giving to others the very grace God had given me.

Ironically, as a Christian, I questioned the faith of Christians more than I had done as an atheist! In searching for a sense of belonging with others, I had found myself belonging less and less.

I had begun to see myself as above others in my understanding of scripture. I couldn't find the mental patience to slow down to everyone else's pace. And spiritually, I was unable to find peace, love, or humility. I thought that if I had to explain, again, to someone that we can only love God because God chose us first, I was going to erupt in a Bible-verse-filled, anger-laced lecture about, ironically, God's grace.

Except, at this point in my life, I didn't see the irony of my arrogance.

Throughout my life, I'd seen things in black and white. I had internalized the binary nature of computer programming and analysis, where something was always either true or false. So when people expressed belief in ideas that contradicted my interpretation of the Bible, I thought it was my duty to point out their error and correct them.

Not surprisingly, I wasn't winning people over to the gospel this way.

Instead, during this darkening phase of my life, I was intent on showing people that I was smarter than them. And making them feel insignificant in the process.

I'm thankful that God had something in store to change my thinking.

※

Throughout this time, I had kept in contact, sporadically, with my father, who was now living on the Gulf Coast of Florida. I loved him, but we didn't have much to talk about, so the phone conversations were few and far between, once every few months.

Then came a fateful call in June 2014, from one of his friends living in the same development. He had just celebrated his 75th birthday in Florida, during the time I was studying Greek back in Pennsylvania.

Even today, thinking about it still brings tears to my eyes.

"Scott," she said, "I believe your father is showing signs of dementia."

This isn't what any son wants to hear, but it was something I had to accept. After several phone calls and a visit later that month to talk with Dad in person, Angie and I decided that it might be good to have him live with us until we sorted out his mental health.

Family takes care of family, we agreed.

One of the first things I did was hop over to Mom's house. Since our move to Lancaster, Angie and I had lived only four miles away, and I wanted to get her thoughts from a medical perspective. She had retired years ago, but she knew first-hand what to expect with dementia patients. What was it going to be like with Dad as he progressed through various stages of the disease?

God teaches us the importance of family throughout the Bible. He wants us to be there for our parents. And it was the right thing to do. I didn't really know Dad as well as I wished I did. This would be an opportunity to bond with him, while we still had time to talk before the dementia took him from me.

I was being given a gift: being able to get to know my father again.

We renovated a summer kitchen on our property for him, turning it into an in-law house. It was a fully functional apartment, with a kitchen (sans oven or stove), bathroom, bedroom, and living room.

As the house was being completed, the doctors confirmed he had early stages of vascular dementia and would experience a slow and steady decline in his health.

Mom told me about something called "sundowning," a reference to increased confusion coming toward the evening. Many people with dementia show more severe symptoms near the end of the day than at the beginning.

It was a sadly appropriate analogy for his long-term diagnosis.

There were seven stages, the neurologist informed us. "Your father has symptoms consistent with stage 3 or early stage 4, showing mild to moderate cognitive decline."

By stage six, my already emotionally distant father would start to have trouble recognizing me.

After laying out the burden we'd have to deal with, the doctor quickly transitioned to talking about living centers that specialized in dementia patients, and presented us with papers describing some nearby locations.

Is he really pushing this right now?

Angie and I had already talked about this. We would watch him. After all, that's why we were fixing up the in-law house.

Being a caregiver was going to be tough, but I knew we could do it. It was the only option in my mind. I had watched Mom care for my grandfather back in 2004 and 2005, when his cancer came back. Family takes care of family. She had taught me that, and it just felt like the right thing to do. I prepared mentally for the next few years.

Mom also did that amazing thing she always did: she told me she'd be there to help if needed. She understood, more than I did at the time, the struggle I would be in for.

※

As Dad's symptoms got worse, the smallest of his habits began to irritate me significantly. It is hard to say if it was his unique idiosyncrasies or it my constant analysis of him that made it more intolerable. By his second year with us, things were becoming much more difficult for me. While I should have been showing him grace, my inexperience with dementia and my obsession with being right made for a volatile mix.

One evening that year, I'd gone over to his living room to eat dinner with him before taking him out bowling. As we sat there, I noticed two stains on the sleeve of his sweatshirt. In truth, it was the third day he'd worn this same outfit, but I thought it best to tread lightly.

"Dad, did you wear that outfit yesterday?" I asked him.

"I don't know," he responded, while sitting back on his recliner.

"What do you mean you don't know?" Just like that, my temper started to fray slightly. "Did you change today, or did you sleep in that?"

"Why do you have to keep asking me the same question over and over again?" His voice was getting more elevated, too.

"Dad, you've got a few stains I recognize from yesterday." I had to prove this to him with facts and point out my observation. My own voice was beginning to rise in volume.

"There you go again, like a broken record. Just leave me alone." He was now yelling.

"Dad, we're going out," I protested. "I just don't want you wearing the same clothes for three days in a row. It's not clean."

Now, I'd admit that I was guilty of occasionally wearing the same thing two days in a row, if it was a lazy weekend. I think my irritation was more about me being embarrassed by him and his stains than the fact he might be wearing the same outfit again. And my pointing it out to him was agitating him.

"Are you saying I'm not clean?" he yelled back at me.

"Dad, it's dirty. You are going to start smelling!"

In just seconds, we had escalated from a simple question to a shouting match. In that moment, I didn't matter that he had dementia. In my mind, I had to get him to come to understand that he still needed to clean himself and change his shirt. *How could he just not get that?*

In the moment, I just wasn't thinking that this is how dementia works. Those with dementia will "mirror" the emotions of those around them. He was only responding to me in the same way I had reacted to him first.

After I stormed out of his living room, I went to my kitchen, made a cup of coffee, then went upstairs to my study and picked out a book from the ceiling-high bookshelf to read. I sat beside the window, staring blankly at the pages of the book while my mind battled with itself.

He was just mirroring me, I thought. *But he had to understand hygiene. But he can't while at this stage of dementia. If kids can learn, so can he.*

I kept going back and forth trying to convince myself that I was right and he was wrong. But I knew better.

I ended up praying hard that night. I prayed differently too.

It wasn't like I was new to prayer at the time. I'd often pray over dinner, pray for people's health, or pray for someone to believe. But on this occasion, I had the first glimmer of reality that I was the one who needed help, not my dad. That I was becoming arrogant, and using my arrogance as a weapon to hide my insecurities.

Praying a prayer for my own humility literally brought tears to my eyes. Where was that sunrise of love from God I'd experienced years before? It was as if the sun was being eclipsed by my own pride, darkening my view of everyone around me.

That night, I felt a warmth come over me. To this day, I still feel that calm when I think of it. It was a soothing and comforting moment. I felt God's love touch me in a way I'd never felt before.

I had a flashback to when I was a kid, how I'd blamed my mom for my own failings, and how she embraced me anyway. I thought of her adopting me despite the fact I'd done nothing to deserve it.

In a way that words still cannot capture, it was a moment where it felt as if God himself was reaching down to embrace me and hold me. A true embrace. It was something I had so needed. Despite my inability to do the same for others, God had showed me what true grace looked like.

※

While I was dealing with Dad's dementia, God led me along a path which I hadn't been expecting, allowing me to help spread his word.

Having his word on my heart and spending time in scripture daily helped me to hear this calling from him and to know that I should trust his plan. It reminds me of what he tells us in John's gospel.

> *"My sheep, they hear the voice of me, and I know them, and they follow me." (John 10:27, personally translated from the Byzantine Greek Text)*

That summer, a former colleague reached out and told me that the theater in Lancaster where he worked was looking for someone with my design talents.

"Scott," he suggested, "Why don't you come over and just take a look at the theater? You might like to see some of what we do here."

He was right.

I felt deep in my heart that God was leading me there to help the theatre's team spread God's word. That fall, they brought me on board full-time as a graphic designer, to be a part of the team that would design upcoming shows.

Working there, I was surrounded by people who trusted God in every aspect of their lives, who placed God first. Seeing how they interacted with others, seeing the grace they showed people, and seeing their connections with others helped me to focus and reflect on my own struggle with feelings of isolation.

Intellectually, I had learned much from my studies of scripture. But emotionally, I still felt that I was struggling to overcome those feelings. I never seemed to be present in the moment, but rather outside it, analyzing everything happening around me.

It was as though, having received God's grace, I was squandering it by treating it like book knowledge instead of building relationships with people.

For me, the biggest obstacle to building relationships was my fear of rejection. I rarely articulated this to anyone other than Angie.

※

I began to think that perhaps, if I could find someone I could connect with on a deeper level besides my wife, I could figure out how to step outside of this mental wall of isolation. I could build relationships with others, support them, and be there for them when they needed it.

There had to be someone besides my wife who would accept me as me. I was doubtful: Angie was a special kind of person. I really had not met anyone like her, and my life had changed so much since we met. But I had to know whether the incredible bond I had with Angie was because of her ability to slip inside that isolation chamber I created, or whether somehow in connecting with her I had taken a few steps outside that wall on my own.

Being able to connect with someone the way I could with Angie might help me answer that question. Or better yet, show me how to overcome that isolated feeling altogether.

This thought evolved and took shape, with some subtle guidance from Angie, around the end of 2017.

"What is it about me?" I finally asked her. "I just feel out of place, so different. I have a hard time building relationships with others. Like no one else besides you really gets me. I just feel so alone sometimes."

She offered several suggestions but then said something I wasn't expecting.

"What about your biological family? I mean, they're your blood. There might be a connection there. And just think about what they might be like."

Interesting, I thought.

"Don't you want to know them?"

"I do. But I don't," I told her. Just thinking about it evoked several emotions.

I mean, if I was rejected by a friend, I could always find a new friend. I had already done that several times in my life. But if my birth mom or birth family rejected me, there would be no other family I could find. That would be it. Game over. So I had taken the safe option and simply convinced myself that not searching for them was the better way. I couldn't be rejected if I didn't reach out.

I had turned my biological family into an unread book on my ever-growing bookshelf filled with potential knowledge. It was as though I was punting as long as I could to delay a potentially bad outcome.

In truth, the thought of my biological family embracing me was tugging at me increasingly. But what if they didn't embrace me? They had already given me up once. And it had been more than four decades since my birth. They had not reached out to me in four decades. Was the reason for that lack of contact that they wanted to keep things that way?

Once I reached out, there would be no turning back. I would need to place all my faith in God to help me. Sure, I could keep ignoring the tug. But that idea of God adopting me and my mom adopting me, both out of love, kept making its way to the front of my thoughts.

"Did my birth mom give me up so I'd be better off, knowing she'd never see me again?" I wondered aloud to Angie. "If that's true, that would mean there's a chance for me to build a bond with her. But, what if that isn't the case? What if it's the opposite?"

My analytical mind had a field day at this point, running every possible outcome through my internal calculator. How would they react to the news that I was contacting them?

"Trust God, Scott," Angie responded. *I wish I could*, was all I could think.

When computers are forced to do too many computations, they get hot. My previous laptop would get so hot when I was editing that I literally couldn't hold it on my lap, it was that uncomfortable. My mind, for years, felt like this. Rarely would I not be analyzing. Self-diagnosing, I attributed my frequent headaches to this analytical overload. The more I internalized my mental turmoil, the worse my headaches got.

For the rest of 2017, I thought more about reaching out to my biological family. I noticed my headaches were becoming more severe and wondered: Was this brought on from knowing I would soon have to make an actual decision about looking for them? Was I simply afraid of their rejection?

"Scott," Angie said to me, "Your mom was young when she had you. That means she likely had more kids. Don't you want to know if you have a brother or sister? Think how much they might be like you!"

What if she was right? My mom would have been young, but how young? If I had a brother or sister, would they be like me? Up until now, I had always felt like I was on a genetic island. The only person like me was me. But was there someone else out there thinking the same thing, wondering about their phantom brother?

But there were all those deep fears of what I might discover to contend with: Was my biological mother happy she had me? Disappointed? Would I feel guilty if she had needed my help but I was too late? *Too late!* Chills. If I was too late, I'd never find those answers.

Angie had a way of nudging me delicately the way an Army private in airborne training is nudged out of a plane on their first jump. When I was about 42, she got me thinking more seriously about DNA tests.

Pieces of my own story were drifting around me. Near the end of 2017, I would bring it up in passing from time to time with my adoptive mom, casually asking for information about my biological family. Other times Angie would ask questions. Fragments of a story about an Italian cruise line. Something about my birth mother being very young when she had me. But these random bits of information would mostly float through my consciousness like figments of a dream, just after waking up. Would a DNA test really bring those threads into focus?

DNA

Growing up, I inherited the culture of my adoptive family. I guess, really, we all do this. Our culture is the culture of our surroundings, and the most prominent of that is our home. So I did what most children did. I celebrated the same holidays that my parents did. I went to the same schools as my family. It's just what we all did.

For much of my life it felt mostly natural, though there were moments when it definitely felt as though I was outside looking into someone else's life.

My adoptive father was Irish. I did love Irish music and culture. And drinking. Back in college, I excelled at that Irish trait, likely too much, even swimming with sharks to do it.

On my adoptive mother's side, there was the German culture. I loved the German side, but it never felt as natural with me, personally. I did look up to many German engineers over the years, especially when it came to problem solving. Facing difficult challenges really pushed me, not just to solve, but to solve in the best way possible. Wernher von Braun, the German aerospace engineer who literally invented rocket science, was a childhood hero (yeah, full nerd status here).

But I never "felt" as German as I thought the rest of my family was. I just felt different, as though those roots didn't run very deep, despite my adoptive family's strong German ties and Lancaster County having such a rich German heritage. (Okay, I have to admit, I did enjoy funnel cakes.)

Even as a junior in high school, in the fall of 1991, when given a choice to follow the path of most everyone else in my family and study German, I opted instead for Latin. Yeah. Latin. I think I reasoned to someone at one point that it would help with my SAT scores. But what high school kid decides to take Latin?

At the time I didn't think much of it. I was just a little different from my family, and I mostly chalked up my detachment to just being weird. Only rarely did I link this sense of being outside the norm to being adopted. Family is family, after all. I loved them, and still do.

The few friends I had were fellow misfits, the ones others called nerds because, instead of excelling in sports, we excelled in intellectual pursuits. Being classified like this never hurt my feelings. Quite the opposite; I took it as a compliment. Anything intellectual, I wanted to conquer.

My mom challenged me early and often. And I ended up excelling because of it. I took and studied the hardest classes. I took calculus and physics a year ahead of everyone else in my grade because I thought it was fun. I was one of a few students to take college-level physics in my high school the first year it was offered. The seven of us jokingly called it Super Physics, to separate us from the "normal" physics class.

But at the same time, I daydreamed more than most, drawing and focusing on art. In a family of engineers, nurses, and schoolteachers, I was the only artist in my family. I floated between the smart kids and the artistic kids, never really fully belonging to either side.

I carried sketchbooks. I drew constantly. My drawings leaned towards a highly detailed and highly, shall I say, odd style. Maybe the meticulous German culture surrounding me did indeed seep into my way of thinking, because I would create drawings that were incredibly detailed. In fact, they were hundreds of drawings in one. On a single sheet of paper, I'd fill every possible inch with scenes woven around and within other scenes, and inside of those yet more. Mountains would be drawn growing out of coffee mugs and odd monkey men with mustaches would peer over their bifocals at a pencil bearing a small army of lemmings. Some of the details were barely large enough to see without a magnifying glass. If you stood back and looked at a collection of my work, you'd be seeing a detailed mosaic of the creative chaos in my mind. So, yeah, I guess I never drew the 'normal' stuff.

What I liked about making art was spending those untold hours just creating it. It wasn't the reward of a finished piece but rather the creative process itself that pulled me in. At the same time, I did want to know where all those thoughts came from.

These questions about ethnicity and heritage and their effects on my life were lurking in the back of my head while I contemplated doing a DNA test to discover a little bit more about who I am. Maybe I'd find a group, a culture, to which I could then belong.

These were the first impulses I had to seriously begin searching for me.

※

For most people, computer programming is like reading the annual congressional budget: lots of boring moments suddenly interrupted by those few special moments of more boring.

But for some reason, I have always loved to code. I'm analytical like that (or as my friends affectionately say, boring). While I started programming on that old computer as a kid, it took on a life of its own, especially in 1994, when I coded much more complicated apps. I wrote a rocket propulsion simulation program in college that calculated the thrust of the engine based on the fuel combustion temperature and changing air density as it climbed higher. Then, when mobile phones started running apps, I wrote programs for that.

As the size of a program, or app, grows, so does its complexity. If you're not careful, all those lines of code can begin to twist and turn, as one block of code tells another block to do something. Programmers call this twisting code, which gets increasingly sloppy and messy, *spaghetti code*. And it isn't a compliment.

It's tough to keep the code as clean as you'd like. Because I was only a part-time programmer, my code in no way resembled an efficient way of thinking. My code was always infused with the well-crafted texture of bloated spaghetti.

Knowing how difficult it is to write clean code gave me the insight to better appreciate it when I saw it. When one looks at computer code (or even a book, like this one) it's clear that someone wrote it. Designed it. It couldn't just write itself on its own from nothing.

Understanding the difficulty of making even a small app do complex things makes DNA, our biological code book for who we are and how we are built, all the more astonishing. DNA is so complex that after decades of mapping it, we are only now beginning to understand how information is coded within it.

For me, there is no doubt that our genetic code book is like any other book: It was written. It didn't just write itself randomly. There is a designer who coded us, built us fiber by fiber, and left our DNA as his fingerprint for us to eventually discover. Psalm 139:13 even tells us how God knit us together in our mother's womb. He cares for us that much.

God knew us before the foundation of the world.

Humans can write our tiny computer apps. God wrote the ultimate app: human life. And it is complex, from its macro-level integration within the biosphere down to the micro level of the smallest proteins. We are complex, created beings, built with DNA.

DNA is almost as complex as learning to kiss.

The amount of data embedded in DNA is staggering. Researchers and companies that offer testing are only now scratching the surface of extracting some of our traits from our DNA. They can tell us all sorts of details, from our ancestral roots to whether or not we like the smell of blue cheese.

For real.

Everything about us is written into our DNA, and some of that is available to us (for a price) from these companies. Just send them a sample of your DNA.

And that right there is where the brakes came on for me, bringing everything to a screeching halt. Knowing how much data you are handing over with a small sample of saliva fueled my concern to protect my DNA from intellectual property theft, as though it was a secret cola recipe.

That might sound paranoid, but consider this: one of the largest consumer DNA websites that decodes your nationality was also closely tied to one of the largest search engines and data storage sites in the world. What would happen if I submitted my DNA to one of these sites? Would my DNA be stored forever? Would I be cloned in another century? Would they own my copyright? Would I end up in some secret government database?

These are serious, long-term issues, and I wasn't the only one asking them as I considered my options. Many privacy and intellectual property questions were being asked in regard to DNA tests. Would knowing some genetic information be worth that potential loss to my privacy? Who in their right mind would send their DNA to be stored in a database, conceivably to be sold to the highest bidder?

Every neuron in my analytical mind said: No! Don't do it!

But then I heard Angie's voice echoing inside my head, too. It was getting louder, drowning out the skepticism. My desire to find out who I am was doing much the same.

Under those two influences, in mid-December 2017, I caved and ordered my DNA kit.

※

The Thursday after Christmas that year was bitterly cold. When my wife opened the front door to check the mail, the freezing cold, 19-degree air sent a shiver down her spine.

"Scott, you got a package in the mail," Angie said to me.

"Well this has to be it. Do we take bets on what I am?" I tried to joke with her.

She rolled her eyes and handed it to me.

The tiny package came in a cardboard box. Opening the well-branded packaging, I read the instructions. Well, I didn't so much read them as glance at some pictures. Amazingly, the instructions for taking a highly scientific and state-of-the-art DNA test had been simplified for our current 140-character generation to just six graphics, with each line drawing inside its own circle, illustrating the steps required to collect a sample of DNA.

Picture one: open and take the small swab out.

I think I can handle this, I thought.

Picture two: swab the inside of the cheek.

I obliged and swabbed my cheek, then followed the next several images to package that bit of saliva in a plastic bio-hazard tube, close it, stuff it into the brown, padded envelope provided, and mail it back.

Well that was easy, I thought. Now I wait.

It seemed like months. But eventually, in early 2018, I received an email saying the results had been analyzed.

What would I find out from the DNA test? At the least, I figured I'd find out something about my ethnicity. And maybe, just maybe, someone from my birth family would have taken a test too, and I'd see a link. Then again, what were the odds that two or three specific people in the world took the same DNA test with the same company?

Had my mother, a possible sibling, or an aunt, uncle, or cousin taken this test with this company? I wasn't holding my breath, figuring it was better to expect that my questions about my mother's identity would remain unanswered.

I knew the odds were high that I would continue to live as a genetic island, never knowing anyone else with my blood-line. No bridge to a genetic parent, sibling, or any other relative who would look like me, think like me, or just be some-what like me.

But deep down, I was still praying to see at the top of the list "Mother" or "Brother" or "Sister" next to a name. Ironi-cally, while I wanted that, I didn't want to find out why I had been given away. Was I given away out of love—or embarrassment?

The login wheel on the website spun as I hit enter, and when the dashboard loaded up, I saw several options.

The first option to click on listed my ethnicity. Two "regions" were listed. The first region said I was just a bit more than half Irish. Okay. Interesting. I wasn't sure why, but I could see that. The other part took me a bit by surprise.

Italian.

Blink. Blink. I had not anticipated this. I was part Italian? For real? I felt my forehead wrinkling in puzzlement. Italian? I guess. It is possible.

At least now loving wine and Latin made some sense. Angie and I had been to Italy, and I was drawn to it for sure. I absolutely fell in love with Milan when we were there for a vacation the year before. But was this the reason why? Was I drawn to my ancestral home? I couldn't understand how that could be hard-wired into a person that way. But, there it was.

Then I saw the next button. The one that would list potential relatives. Clicking it could unlock the answers to so many questions I had been asking myself for years. It also could also generate more questions. Or it could say nothing and leave me wanting.

The cursor blinked off and on slowly but steadily. Taunting me to click the button.

So, taking a deep breath, I clicked it. Would I finally see a name or picture of my mother, father, or even a sibling? That next page began to load on my computer screen.

And then the list populated.

As much as I had secretly hoped for some major discovery, it wasn't to be. The closest relative estimated by my DNA analysis was a distant second or third cousin. Some guy named "Bob."

Bad Bob

At first, I didn't think much about this new relative. On one hand, this was the first time I had ever been presented with a link to someone who was directly related to me, albeit distantly. But would that distance become a highway to my immediate family, or a chasm?

Additionally, I started thinking of the protocol for contacting long lost biological families who might or might not want to be found. Was there such a protocol?

My mind started racing through potential conversations. I could see it play out pretty clearly.

"Hi, so, yeah. You don't know me. But over four decades ago, one of your aunts, or a distant cousin (I don't know which one), had a baby out of wedlock, then gave him up for adoption while keeping it on the down low. By the way, I don't even know her name. And MY name isn't going to be a help because I only know my adopted name. So you get no hints."

And that was assuming that my biological mother *wanted* to be found. There was always the very real possibility that she didn't want anyone knowing about that inconvenient part of her past. Having some stranger asking around wouldn't just be awkward; shedding light on deep dark secrets could potentially rip apart a family. I wanted to tread very carefully.

But nonetheless, the challenge remained that he was such a distant relative. With a first cousin, I could more easily find family who was the right age to be my mom. But nope. Even if Bob could help, he was a second or third cousin and the next few people on the list were fourth and fifth cousins.

At that point I'd have better luck driving to Boston and asking random strangers. At least I knew that should I drive to Boston, though the chances of finding my birth mother were pretty much zero, I could at least find a fresh lobster dinner.

Thankfully, while I was trying to figure out how to do this, Bob himself reached out in an email that spring. The email chats with Bob began somewhat slowly. But as we talked, I realized how interested he was in helping me and we emailed much more frequently. We had some incredible conversations in the process. I learned more about his background, and he listened to the hints I had about my birth mom.

As the conversations went on, I realized how much this distant cousin knew, including stories about a family whiskey distillery a few generations ago. He started telling me details about distant relatives of his that could be my mother or grandparents. And he got a kick out of telling me that he had built a reputation such that people called him *Bad Bob*.

Okay, I thought. *Who is this guy?*

Then, in what might be the most buried lede ever, in one email he asked causally, "So, would you like me to share access to my genealogy tree?"

I said sure, thinking it would be fun to dig around and see what he had found. When I had tried out a free trial for the same genealogy site years earlier, I entered maybe 20 names of people I knew. It was fun for a few days. But that was it. So I wasn't expecting much this time around.

In hindsight, his comment was closer to having a guy tell you he works at a library, only to discover he's the director of the Library of Congress.

The curtain had been pulled back. And the more I browsed, the more trails I discovered. His tree literally had over 16,000 names, all of them people he was related to.

How did this guy have so much information on so many people?

How *bad* was Bad Bob?

I found not just birthdays and death dates, as applicable, but what towns they had lived in, photos for many, and so much more. The trees went up for generations. Within a few clicks, I was able to go back more than five centuries, in Bob's direct maternal or paternal lineage. He had traced lines back to the 1500s, including brothers and sisters; first, second and third cousins; and multiple marriages and the spouses' children and parents.

How could one guy get this much data? He had told me how he was analytical and loved finding links in ancestry and genealogy, and he just wanted to know more about his family.

Hobby or not, it was beginning to feel like I had tapped into some secret military database on every citizen and my house was about to be raided as the government traced the signal to my laptop.

Even with this incredible resource now available to me, I still wasn't sure where to look. There were so many names and so few clues. Yet Bad Bob helped out anyway, in whatever way he could. He and I kept looking at potential family members that would be the right age and at the right location. For weeks, we kept exploring possible branches in his family tree.

Despite his nickname, Bad Bob had turned out to be one of the kindest and most helpful people I had ever met. I told him that I'd have to make the two-hour drive to meet him in person once this was all said and done. For now, though, we continued to email clues back and forth as we dug deeper to find my birth mom.

Even though he and I ran into dead ends, he continued to look for links for me, while telling me incredible stories from his own family. This was an amazing family, for sure. It was an interesting search, but I was missing details.

I needed to go to my adoptive mom for more information on my birth mom. She knew I had done the DNA test, and she knew I had received my nationality results, telling me I'm mostly Irish and Italian. And I had told her the closest link was a distant cousin. Now I was going to tell her about Bad Bob, and I'd have to be more direct with my questions to her about my birth family.

It took me several days to build up the courage to ask Mom for help. To be honest, I was afraid of what she would think, and I certainly didn't want to hurt her feelings. But at the same time, I couldn't stop thinking about what my biological parents were like.

I had to know.

Finally, one Thursday evening in late June, while sitting at home in my office upstairs, I picked up my phone and called

Mom. I shouldn't have been nervous as I heard it ringing, but there I was, getting butterflies in my stomach, afraid of offending or hurting her just by asking what I was about to ask.

"Good evening," Mom answered. "How are you?"

"I'm good," I said, then paused, building up the strength to put the question out there. Once I did let it out, I could barely breathe.

"I had a question for you. I've been in touch with someone I met on the DNA site. He's a third or fourth cousin according to our DNA. He has been very nice in trying to help me search through his family tree to find any closer relatives. But there's just too many names in his family tree to narrow it down. Do you happen to have my birth certificate? Something with my birth mom's name on it?"

I paused. I assumed this would be hard for her to talk about and I wasn't sure what to expect. What she said next surprised me.

"Well, I can tell you that your birth certificate doesn't have her name on it. It has my name on it and Dad's name. I have a copy of it around here somewhere."

I discovered later that she was right. It had been so long since I had seen my birth certificate to get my passport that it slipped my mind. I was also surprised to learn that I had two birth certificates. The one Mom had was my Amended Birth Certificate. It was created after my adoption had been completed and had my adoptive mom and dad's name. However, I also had an Original Birth Certificate. This one was locked away in Boston's Registry of Vital Records and was unavailable for me to view without a court order. This certificate would be the one that had my birth mother's name on it. But at this point in my search, I had no idea I had two different certificates.

So I abandoned this option for the time being and asked if she had any information that might help.

"Hmm. Don't worry about digging that out then. Do you happen to remember her name?"

"I don't know her name," my mom answered. "I never met her. All I remember is her father's last name."

"Anything would help. What was it?"

"He was an engineer just outside of Boston," she said. And then my mom started naming a bunch of letters. After the third letter I realized she was spelling his last name. I quickly jotted the name down on a piece of paper.

"That might help," I said before thanking her and saying good night.

On the one hand, I worried that she had spelled it out instead of saying it because she was hesitant to even speak the name out loud. On the other hand, I knew she understood how important this was for me and gave it to me to help. Still …

Did she feel the same disappointment and sadness as the father of the prodigal son when asked for his inheritance? Did she now think I wanted to say my goodbye to her family in search of a new family?

I had to let her know that wasn't my intention. I redialed her number.

"Did you find them that fast?" she asked, half-joking.

"Ha. Right." I half-joked back, trying to lighten the mood. "I just wanted to say I love you and thank you for helping. This means a lot."

We talked for a few more minutes and I made a mental note to make a very strong effort to continue making that fact clear over the next few weeks. Even on the unlikely possibility that I found my birth mom, or had the chance to meet her, the mom I grew up with was always going to be my Mom. Never anything less. I wanted to make sure she knew that, too.

※

It wasn't until I hung up with her that second time that I really stared at that name on the paper. At that moment, I felt a thud in my chest. That enormous sound of nothing coming from my office was me.

I had seen that name before.

My mind raced backward and forward as though scrubbing through a recording on a reel-to-reel player, searching for that one lost bit of something that was familiar enough to recall, but lost enough that I didn't know where to look for it. It took me a good minute or two before I could think clearly enough to just let my computer search for me.

I searched back through Bob's emails and sure enough, there it was. He had brought up that last name as one in a short list to investigate. Had I skipped this name by accident?

I logged back into his genealogy tree to double-check. That's when I saw it. Staring me right in the face, like one of those posters that first appear to be nothing but a mass of dots, teasing you to let your eyes go out of focus enough to spot the image of a spaceship. Except that now, I didn't have to cross my eyes to see it. It was right there.

My grandfather's name.

But Bob's family tree didn't have a daughter listed for my grandfather - only a son. That's why I had passed over them earlier in my search. Bob told me he had conversed with the son. This meant that this person, my grandfather's son, was my uncle.

My uncle!

My mind quickly jumped back two steps. Bob had told me he had actually spoken with my uncle. Six degrees of separation suddenly imploded to a single name on a computer screen. So Bob's tree had both my grandfather and my uncle; he just hadn't uncovered yet that my grandfather had a daughter, too.

At that moment, time stopped. As I stared at the family tree, my imagination envisioned another square slowly appearing under my grandfather's name and next to my uncle. But there was no name to fill that empty square, the one that belonged to my mother.

I had to know.

I opened up a new browser window and sat staring at the search engine page as I thought about my next step. Do I open up a social media site and see if my uncle has a presence there? Do I email Bob and see about getting in touch with my uncle? Then it hit me. Could it be that simple?

In the search field, I slowly typed my grandfather's name and the city where I was born. I hit search.

I can't remember the last time I used an actual yellow pages or white pages telephone book. Everything's online now, and fast. Would a digital white page pull it off?

Sure enough. The first search result was a direct hit. I clicked to the white page. There it was: my grandfather's name, plus an address, and even an age and a few possible related names, one of which was my uncle's name from Bob's tree.

The age on this white pages listing matched what Bob had. The address was the right town. *Could it be him?*

And below that were two women's names. One had an address from the town where I was born, just outside of Boston.

Laura.

Was that her? Was Laura my mom? My aunt? Who was she?

It was already about 3 or 4 a.m. Friday morning, and I was still wide awake.

The genealogy website Bob and I were using also allowed us to search old yearbooks and newspaper articles. I typed the first woman's name into the site's search engine and got a hit on a high school senior yearbook.

Clicking on it, I pulled up the picture: a black-and-white shot of a young girl with straight, dark hair, looking off to the side, smiling.

For the first time in my life, I looked at a picture and saw someone who looked related to me. We had similar cheeks, a similar smile, and similar eyes.

She was family. But what part? Was she my mother? Was she an aunt?

I realized that, since I was pulling an all-nighter, there was a good chance this was just my imagination playing tricks on me. Or worse, I had fallen asleep at my desk and would wake up with a sore neck and realize this was all just a dream.

But morning came and it was still there. A picture of this high school senior that sort of looked like me. I woke up my wife and asked her to look at it. She rubbed her eyes, sat up, looked at it. As an artist, Angie spends so much time looking at faces that she can usually pinpoint someone's nationality just from their face. She's like a forensic scientist in that way, picking out tiny details us normal people miss.

"Scott," she said, "that's got to be your mom."

Still, I wanted a second opinion or two. I saved the photo to my phone and went to work.

My search for my biological family had become a part of regular conversation with my friends at work, and when I began showing them this photo, they agreed she was definitely a close relative.

I had to reach out to her and see if she would be able to make the final connection. Sitting at my desk, I pondered how to do this, and all my trepidation came forward again.

What if she isn't my mom?

What if she is, but she doesn't want anyone knowing about me?

These questions still kept racing through my head. Independence Day was that upcoming Wednesday. Was I about to set some unwelcome fireworks off in this family? I prayed a long prayer that I wouldn't destroy a family. I also prayed to God that if it was his will, that this might even be my family.

Without asking there was no way to know exactly who Laura was. There was a chance she was my biological mom, but I couldn't assume that. She could be an aunt, I thought.

I grabbed a piece of typing paper and a pencil and wrote a letter.

Who Writes Letters Anymore?

"Who writes letters anymore?" Laura remembers asking as she looked at the handwritten note that came in the mail that Tuesday morning, that first week of July. It had her name written neatly in block letters in black ink on the front of the envelope.

Her father recently moved in with her and he would routinely walk to the end of the driveway each morning to get the mail.

This Tuesday was no different, except that one piece of mail, among many addressed to Laura, was out of the ordinary: hand-written, with a very particular name on the return address that evoked a very particular reaction. It was as though his mind had been put in one of those bank tubes and been shot with a *thwump* through the vacuum tube filled with memories and colors and pictures of his life, shooting past everything until a second *thwump* landed him back on a crisp and windy January morning, more than four decades earlier.

The name on the envelope was the name of the baby he had held on that chilly January morning. He hurried back to the house.

"Someone wrote you a letter," he called to his daughter, Laura.

"A letter? Who writes letters anymore?" Laura asked. *Letter writing is a lost art,* she thought. Who would write her a letter? Hardly anyone takes the time to hand write a letter these days. She looked at the return label.

"Scott Sullivan? Who's Scott Sullivan?" She looked up at her dad, and saw in his face that he knew who it was. Was it one of his friends? If so, why were they writing a letter to her and not him?

Laura was exceptionally good with details. She was smart and could manage lots of details in her head very well. Some might say she was as smart as a rocket scientist.

Calling someone a rocket scientist is a way for average people to call someone smart. But usually they mean normal-smart. Not *literally* smart enough to design something that goes into space. Only exceptional people do that.

But in this case, they'd be right. She could do that. She had done that, and one of those things she sent into space was now passing the dwarf planet Pluto, formally known as the planet Pluto. Yeah, that Pluto.

Yet she still couldn't place the name.

"It's HIM. Your sister's son."

Time did that time stopping-thing again, this time for Laura. If you've never experienced it before, it's like the entire universe shrinks to the size of an almond. Then floats for a moment. Then cracks ever so slightly. Then instantly expands back to its normal size.

Is it really HIM? She opened the envelope to read the letter and a color photo fell out: someone with dark but graying hair, smiling at whoever was taking his picture.

She didn't recall ever seeing this person before, yet he looked oddly familiar. Oddly similar to her and her sister, and several other family members. His eyes were just like theirs. His smile looked like her sister's. The similarities were uncanny.

Could it really be?

She read my letter.

I had spent some time agonizing over writing and rewriting this letter. How could I say, *I think we are so closely related that you might be my mom or aunt*, but not actually say that on the chance that she was neither. Or, even more sensitively, that she *was* but didn't want anyone to know about me.

I wrote that she and I were biologically related "somehow" through a DNA test I had performed. Then I mentioned the family tree from Bob. I said I was looking for my biological mother and asked if there was any way Laura would be able to help. I thanked her for her time and left my phone number and email.

For good measure, I included the picture, in case there was any resemblance to her.

When I wrote the letter, I wasn't sure how much time would be needed to process this information. News like that might take weeks or months to digest and might require even longer to decide how to respond, if at all. So I left several ways of contacting me in case she wanted to politely send a note or email back saying, nope, she can't help, but good luck.

My deepest fear was that this letter would be discovered by a husband or child who didn't know about me and set off those emotional fireworks.

While my letter did set off fireworks, I could never have imagined anything like the explosions that followed. It all happened faster than anyone could have anticipated, igniting a chain reaction of excitement that couldn't be stopped.

"What do I do?" Laura asked her father. This was him! There were just too many similarities in my face to deny it.

She immediately tried calling her sister. No answer. Susan worked at a major hospital in Florida where it was difficult to simply stop what she was doing to take a call. She loved it at the hospital, with so many challenges to solve as part of her job, often reporting directly to the C-level executives. But she was busy during the day with her many responsibilities, and answering a personal call was next to impossible. Her family knew this.

Susan glanced at her phone and saw that her sister, Laura, was calling her. She knew her sister had taken the week off for Independence Day, and thought Laura must have forgotten that she was still working this week. She'd call her back later.

A few minutes later the phone buzzed again.

Really, Laura? You should know I'm working, she thought. She hit decline a second time.

Laura's excitement was growing, and she needed to reach Susan. She'd have to get ahold of Susan's two daughters to tell them to call their mom.

Christina, Susan's youngest daughter, would typically text her mom and sister throughout the week. They were close and constantly in touch, usually through texts. But Christina, knowing her mom's responsibilities at work, respected her time.

Getting a random text or call first thing in the morning was pretty normal for Christina. Getting a call from her grandfather this morning was a little out of the routine, but not exactly unusual. What he said, though, most certainly was unexpected.

"The Eagle has landed!" he told her, his voice full of excitement.

What? Christina thought to herself. He continued.

"We just got a letter and picture in the mail from your brother."

Christina had, unbeknownst to me, been searching for me for years, turning up one empty lead after another. Each person she contacted who got back to her said: Sorry, but no. He was not her brother.

Years of searching without success can begin to wear on anyone. It's like playing the lottery and never winning. Until one day, the numbers slowly being announced on television keep matching the numbers on your ticket. You just don't expect it. And if it finally happens, you begin to question it. You wonder: Am I awake? Is this a prank? Is this for real?

She was awake. Okay. Not a dream. She wasn't hearing things. Her grandfather had said it very clearly. Could it really be him after all these years?

Christina's eyes began to tear up. Her mind raced. She wanted to read the letter. She wanted to see the picture. She wanted to tell her mom. She wanted to call her brother.

As much as she was dying to speak to me on the phone, Christina's unselfish nature kicked in. She thought her mom should be the first to make that connection. So she waited. Anxiously. But she waited.

Christina sent a text to her mom, telling Susan to call Aunt Laura. Across town, Christina's older sister, Sarah, also received a text from Laura, setting off almost the same sequence of thoughts.

Then the flurry of texts began to grow exponentially as Laura filled her own brothers in on the news.

I can almost picture a poor guy working on network data traffic monitoring for a broadband carrier sitting up in alarm at this moment, with his monitor showing an abnormal spike in bandwidth use on the east coast, stretching from Boston to Miami.

Susan's phone buzzed again. This time from Christina. Almost immediately it buzzed again, from Sarah.

What's going on? What's so important that the whole family is trying to reach me? Her thoughts went from puzzled to worried. Was something wrong with her father? *Is Dad okay?*

Faster than she knew it, she was dialing Laura, dreading the worst. "What's going on, is everything okay?"

"Susan. I got a letter from Scott. I got a letter from your son!"

Thwump happened again.

"What do we do, Susan?" Laura asked. Would Susan call him? Could she? Even with as seismic an event as this, Susan worked in an area of the hospital where, like with air traffic controllers, you can't just take a break and let everything go on autopilot. This was huge news, but her hands were tied at the moment.

"Call him," Susan told her sister. "Talk to him. Tell him about us!"

Just like that, it was settled. Laura would make the call. She would be the first person from the family to talk to her sister's son.

She dialed the number at the bottom of her nephew's letter. It rang a few times, then she heard the line connect.

"Hello, this is Scott."

"Scott. This is Laura. You wrote me a letter."

Hello, This is Scott

I had one more day of work at the theater before the Fourth of July. This year the holiday fell on a Wednesday, so it was two days of work, one day off, then two days on again. Not your normal work week, but in a few hours it became even less so. Which is hard to do, considering that my job is extremely not normal.

I design highly detailed stage sets and animations using software similar to what's used for special effects in feature films. It's a highly artistic and technical job that I knew was right up my alley the moment it was offered.

Sight & Sound Theatre holds 2,000 people per show, with 11 shows per week. The productions include computer-controlled set pieces that can be 30 to 40 feet tall and move across the stage. The "backdrop" is a 113-by-30-foot LED wall that displays photorealistic animated videos which our team creates.

In addition, we have all sorts of live animals on stage as part of the production: everything from horses and sheep to llamas and camels, depending on what the story calls for. Each morning I walk past our animal barn. Some days I see the horses outside being brushed by the trainers in preparation for the show. Other days, the goats or llamas are out in their large pen beside the barn, grazing in their fenced enclosure.

A few steps to the right of the animal barn is where I enter the downstairs level of the massive storage warehouse and fabrication shop, towering several stories over me. Just inside is where I spend my day, part of an amazingly gifted team that designs those videos, animations and set pieces for each upcoming show.

But my favorite thing about the shows is that each one is based on biblical stories, brought to life live on stage. All to spread the gospel and tell God's story.

So needless to say, it's not quite your normal job.

As I was getting my second cup of coffee that morning, casually talking to a few friends at work, that flurry of text messages was flying between Boston to Florida and back, all talking about me. My ear itched.

I went back to my standing desk and took a sip of my coffee, completely unaware that my face was, at that very instant, being transmitted to my mother, sisters, aunts and uncles.

One more sip. Phone calls were now being made about me. My letter was being read a second and third time.

I hit *save* on the design I was working on at that moment and was about to take another sip when my cell phone buzzed. I looked at the caller ID. It wasn't anyone I recognized. But the origin city was in Massachusetts.

My heart skipped a beat. Had she gotten my letter that fast? I slid my finger on the glass screen to answer.

"Hello, this is Scott," I said as I walked away from my desk, going outside to take the call.

I had hardly made it fifteen feet when the woman on the other end replied, "Scott, this is Laura. You wrote me a letter."

※

It's commonplace to say your heart races when you get excited or nervous. But it's a subjective saying. What could be just a slightly raised heart rate could be perceived as a racing heartbeat. On this morning, I was wearing my Apple Watch, which, in addition to logging my steps, sending me email notifications, and so on, records my heart rate. It lets me go back and analyze my health, including what my heart rate was at specific times of the day. I work out quite a bit, so I have a relatively low resting heart rate.

When I went back to look at the data for this particular morning, I noticed that my resting rate just before the call was around 50 beats per minute. According to the health logs stored by my watch, during the first few minutes of this particular call, at 9:07 a.m., July 3, my heart rate almost doubled to 98 beats per minute.

Yeah. My heart was racing.

After a short walk on that cool July morning, I found myself standing outside my office, talking with Laura, as a llama stood near the wooden fence watching me. The llama tilted his head curiously.

"Yes, it's a pleasure to hear from you, Laura. Thank you for calling," I somehow managed to say, stumbling over my words in excitement.

This was all happening much faster than I had anticipated. A friend had told me that I should prepare for the very real possibility that I might not hear back from her for a year, if at all. A friend had just gone through this, and it had taken his biological father a year to process this connection and get back to his son. Some people just take longer to digest this type of news.

Well that digested pretty quickly, I thought.

Her voice seemed upbeat.

That's a good sign, I thought, feeling less worried that I was about to be told never to contact this family again. But who was she? Was this my mom? Or an aunt? Or someone else?

Laura read back to me what I had written: that I was looking for my biological family, including my mother. Almost as quickly as she had repeated the question, she answered it by telling me I hit the bull's-eye.

What? What did she mean by that?

Laura continued. I could hear the elation in her voice. She said: "Scott, I'm your aunt. My sister is your mother."

My. Sister. Is. Your. Mother.

Thwump.

I wasn't sure if I was going to fall down in a faint or shout for joy. Every time I think back to that moment, this first call, my eyes begin to tear up with joy.

There are some things you just can't prepare yourself for in life. This was one of those moments. And what was amazing - what still amazes me to this day - is that God gave me an enormous blessing by allowing me to experience that moment three times in a row.

The first time was hearing from my aunt and her telling me about my mother. Then, just to drive the moment home, I was given another just like it.

"And Scott, you have two sisters."

Thwump.

I had considered the possibility that I had siblings, but had never really thought that through to its logical conclusion. Even though it had always been possible, and even likely, it just wasn't something that felt real before this moment. Logically, it might have been realistic, but emotionally, it felt like a made-up story someone might tell.

Hearing her say those words was like waking up from a dream and seeing the foggy vision of someone standing before you pop into perfect clarity. The idea that I had sisters was no longer just a realistic possibility. It was real.

Sarah and Christina.

What were they like? Were they anything like me? Did they look like me? Did they think like me?

As all of these possibilities raced through my head, Laura let me experience that heart-stopping moment all over again with a third comment.

"And your grandfather is sitting right here. He's so excited to talk with you."

Thwump.

My grandfather!? Everything I had known was changing. In a matter of minutes I had gone from sipping coffee at work to speaking to my aunt, and discovering my mom, my sisters, and now my grandfather.

And he was *excited* to talk with me. Not ashamed. Not angry. Excited.

This was huge. As I had begun searching for my family, that fear of them not wanting to talk with me had grown steadily. The fear that they abandoned me and wanted nothing to do with me grew with each step closer I got to finding my family.

But my own grandfather was *excited* to talk with me. That one comment was the first to quell those fears. Right then, I realized my fear of being alone and isolated might actually be conquered, depending how this all played out.

The line went quiet for a moment as she handed the phone over to my grandfather.

"Scott," he said in a such a way I could tell he was smiling from ear to ear. "Scott, the eagle has landed! My family is complete again."

As my grandfather was talking (he told me to call him Grampy right then and there), I noticed how immediately comfortable it was talking with him. I realized then that I had felt the same thing with Laura. There were no awkward moments or forced conversation. Everything we talked about flowed as though we had known each other for years and were just catching up.

I had gone from having a fear of rejection to being completely comfortable and relaxed talking with my family. *My family!*

My grandfather later reflected on those moments after I was born, back on that January morning in 1975. His description was so vivid, so burned into his memory, that I could tell it had been deeply emotional.

"Scott," he said, "for years when people asked how many grandchildren I had, I always included you as one of them. When you were born and we had to give you away, I was the last person to hold you before handing you over for the adoption. You have no idea how happy I am that this day finally came."

After we'd talked for a while, he gave the phone back to my aunt - Auntie Laura, as I'd call her from that point on. She explained how much my mother was dying to talk me and that she would be calling me that evening.

Auntie Laura told me my mother had moved from Boston to Florida more than twenty years ago, when her daughters - my sisters - were very young.

Then she told me more about my sisters. How hard Christina had been searching for me, how eager she was to talk with me, and that I'd probably be hearing from both her and Sarah soon.

She told me Sarah had just graduated from nursing school. Christina had just gotten married late last year. I had missed both of these huge moments by months.

Realizing that gave me a sharp emotional punch: *I should have started this sooner.* I could have been there to see Christina get married. I could have been at Sarah's nursing graduation. What else had I missed? But then again, there was so much to look forward to.

My mom was going to call me later. My sisters were going to be calling me too!

When Auntie Laura said I'd hit the bull's-eye, she was right. This phone call was changing everything.

I started to hope that talking with my mom and sisters would be as easy as it was to talk with my aunt and grandfather. Would I get along with them? What if they didn't like me? The doubts still floated to the surface.

Finally, we wrapped up our conversation, and Auntie Laura once more told me how thrilled they were to finally reconnect. I told her how excited I was and that I couldn't wait until we could meet in person.

My mind raced. *Meet! I can't wait to meet them!* Boston's only about a six-hour drive. I could do that easily.

But my mom and sisters were in Florida. I knew then and there that I was going to have to take a few days off from work and hop on a plane to visit them. As much as I wanted to meet Auntie Laura, Florida had to be the first trip. Laura agreed. And, she said, she wanted to fly down to Florida to be there for this!

After I hung up, I stood there, staring at my phone, overwhelmed by what had just happened. The llama just stared.

※

I went back inside and, within moments, commented to a close friend: "I just spoke to my aunt."

I was on the verge of laughing and crying at the same time.

Within minutes everyone was over listening, eager to hear me recap my conversation. While I was sharing the news with my workmates, the story continued to develop. Auntie Laura had begun texting me a series of photos. The first was of my mom and grandfather. The next two were my sisters, each with their husbands and kids.

Later that Tuesday evening, my phone rang with an unknown number from Florida.

"Hello, this is Scott."

"Scott, this is Susan. It is so amazing to talk to you!"

It was my birth mom. After more than four decades, we were finally able to talk. I could hear the joy in her voice as she spoke. I kept bouncing back and forth between feeling overwhelmed and being in disbelief. But her voice was real. She was real.

"So," I said. "How are you?" I really wasn't sure what to ask or how. I had so many questions. I wanted to know so much and had no idea where to start. Yet, as the conversation went on, I didn't feel hesitant, or afraid of saying the wrong thing. There was no awkward silence with either of us not knowing what to say. Quite the opposite. It was as if I was trying to cram four decades' worth of questions through my cell phone's tiny microphone.

"I'm soooo good," she responded. "Thank you, thank you, thank you for calling. I'm so happy you did. We were afraid you didn't want anything to do with us."

I was stunned to find out my mom had harbored the same fear I had held for so many years. I was afraid she wanted nothing to do with me and that this was the reason she never reached out to me. She was afraid that I had decided to turn my back on her because she had given me up for adoption. Neither could have been further from the truth.

Reflecting on that, I could only imagine how many people in the world go years without speaking to others because of false assumptions about the other's attitude.

"I'm so glad I did, too," I said. "I was afraid you didn't want to hear from me. God guided us to eventually get here, on this call right now."

Talking about God and his sovereignty in all things is so natural for me, I sometimes forget how naturally he becomes part of my conversation. I think of Proverbs 16:33 often, where we are told *"every decision is from the LORD."* And in one of my favorite letters, Paul's letter to the Ephesians, he describes God as *"working all things according to the purpose of his will." (Ephesians 1:11, personally translated from the Byzantine Greek Text)*

That it took me this long to connect with them, I trusted, was part of God's design. He knew I simply wasn't ready to meet them earlier in my life. But as I said this, it occurred to me that I had no idea if they even believed in God.

Yet she agreed. "It's his perfect timing," my mom said back. How true. I breathed a sigh of relief that she and her family also trusted in God's sovereignty.

We spoke for a while longer, talking about everything from my mom's health (to reassure me that I didn't have any genetic surprises to worry about), to my sisters and their husbands and kids.

We eventually wrapped up our first phone call, knowing we'd be talking much more over the next days and weeks. Over the next few days, my sisters took turns calling me. And with every new conversation I felt more like Alice falling down the rabbit hole. Yet, just like Alice drinking tea, it was still oddly familiar and normal.

I knew all of this was huge and normally would be overwhelming. But somehow, while talking with Auntie Laura, Grampy, then my mom, Christina, and Sarah, I felt comfortable. It felt normal. They didn't feel like strangers, though I had only spoken with them briefly. They felt like family.

Then it struck me. They *were* family.

As the week progressed and we all talked, we found a weekend two weeks out that would work for us all to meet. I booked two plane tickets for Angie and me. We were about to take a trip to southern Florida.

As the countdown began to meet my family face to face, my mom, in one of our telephone conversations, told me about my biological father. Up until this point, all I knew was there was something involving an Italian cruise ship. I also knew my mom was young when she had me.

"It all happened because I got on the honor roll," my mother said. "My father, your Grampy, wanted to give me a great high school graduation gift for doing so well. My father surprised me by coming into my room one weekend and saying I earned it. He told me he was going to take me on a cruise because of my grades."

I listened to her tell the story and tried to picture everything she told me.

An Italian Souvenir

"You earned it," Susan's father said smiling, as he handed her a ticket for an Italian cruise. Susan was graduating from high school, with honors, that spring in 1974. Her father turned to Susan's younger brothers and sister and said, "And, if you do as well in high school, like your sister, I'll take you on a cruise also."

But this was a trip that would change several lives forever.

In April 1974, Susan and her parents left their small suburban house just outside Boston and flew to Florida. As they arrived at the port in Fort Lauderdale, Susan looked up and saw the Italian flag on the ship they were about to board. The *Fairwind* was one of two new cruise ships from Sitmar, recently commissioned out of San Marco shipyards in Trieste, Italy.

And there it was at the dock, with a mass of passengers walking across the gangways. Hundreds were already standing against the railings of the ship, drinking cocktails, ready to watch the ship make way.

That's a massive ship, Susan thought. *I'm going to have so much fun on this trip!*

She had just turned 18, and this was her first big trip. Susan was given a great deal of flexibility to go off on her own while they were at sea, as long as she checked in with her father at specific times.

While exploring, Susan ran from one activity to another. She was a free spirit who loved meeting new people. She'd constantly be striking up conversations with other passengers and crew members.

As this was an Italian ship, most of the crew had names that ended with the letters *o* and *i*. One of the crew members in particular—I'll call Mr. F—caught Susan's attention.

Mr. F was from near Milan, at the foot of the snow-capped mountains of northern Italy. He was taller than her, with dark hair and blue eyes. And, oh, that Italian accent.

Susan found herself attracted to him. And each day, they spent more time together.

The ship spent considerable time at sea, giving passengers a generous amount of free time. One evening, the two of them strolled to one of the upper decks of the cruise ship to watch the sun set over the waters.

The sky that spring evening was filled with gold, pink and orange bands against the few clouds on the horizon. High above, the colors slowly faded to a dark blue, where the stars began to twinkle, accompanied by the sound of ocean swells and the low hum of the engine far beneath.

Susan and the Italian stood there and took in the view for awhile until they went off to explore the ship, enjoy the music and party.

Susan picked up several souvenirs on this trip. But the most memorable one, the one that would hold far more sentimental value than everything else on this cruise, was the one she failed to declare to customs on her return to Fort Lauderdale.

In fact, she didn't discover it until several weeks after their return to Boston. This Italian souvenir wouldn't be born until nine months later.

※

The mid-'70s were a great time for a free spirit like Susan. But the reality of what it would take to raise a child at such a young age weighed heavily on her mind. Back in New England, she kept in touch with Mr. F for a while, but it just was not meant to be.

Distance made it hard. And they were both aware of just how wide the Atlantic was, and it gradually overcame this relationship. Their relationship was over.

As the summer of 1974 began in New England, my mom did what she could to hide her pregnancy while the other students from her senior class were out celebrating their graduation and taking in the summer, going to Castle Island to enjoy the beach in South Boston, and similar activities.

She would skip those days, instead lying awake at night, trying to figure out what would be the best thing to do for herself and her child.

She thought a lot about college. Would this baby mean she wouldn't have the time to commit to college? Could she possibly give this baby the needed attention? There was no way she could properly take care of this baby and herself. And there would be so many sacrifices, for both of them.

Fall weather crept up on Boston quickly, the leaves turning to browns, reds, and oranges earlier than normal that year.

Personally, fall is my favorite season. Every year, I look forward to getting my sweaters and scarves out and walking in the brisk outdoor air. There is something magical in hearing the leaves crunch beneath my feet while the early evening sun gives the streets a warm, amber glow.

But back then, while I was still months from being born, my mom was looking at fall from a vastly different perspective. She knew she wouldn't be able to give her baby the life she wanted for him or her. The best life for me, she was coming to conclude, would be to give me up for adoption to a family who could care for me in a way she couldn't.

And as this reality set in, fall, for her, became cold and hard. The reds, oranges, and browns painting the landscape were signs of an end. The life she had dreamt of before she was pregnant was dying day by day, as the chilled air drained the warmth from her life.

In a few months, I'd be gone, and this part of her life would be over.

She tried to console herself with the thought that at least I would be able to have a full life. I'd have a new life with a family that could provide what she couldn't.

Sure enough, just south of Boston, in the small town of Milton, a married couple in their mid-thirties had been looking to raise a family and were actively looking to adopt.

My adoptive mom-to-be, Karen, had graduated as a nurse about ten years earlier and had been doing well working at one of the largest teaching hospitals in Boston.

My adoptive dad-to-be was an electrical engineer who had started as a lineman out in the field and risen in the ranks quickly - partly because he wanted to make more money and partly because working outside on electrical lines during Boston's frigid winters made you want to get a desk job. Fast.

Regardless, they were financially well-placed to bring a little one into their home.

During the latter part of fall, one of Karen's friends, who knew she was looking to adopt, mentioned that he knew a young woman from the north end of Boston who was looking to give a baby up for adoption. This baby hadn't even been born yet, he told her.

Now, most adoptions take place through an agency. Mine, however, began through this mutual friend who knew both families. And during the last few months of 1974, the adoption paperwork was finalized.

Now they just had to wait for *me* to be finalized.

※

The second Saturday of the new year was an ordinary January morning for most Bostonians. Windy and bitter, the air just above freezing, with frost still covering car windows. But for some, it was an extraordinary day. Myself, especially.

I was born.

This occasion brought tears from two families. Tears of joy from one, and sadness from the other. I was, of course, ignorant of all that. But even had I been able to comprehend it, I saw none of it.

Back in the '70s, there was a fear that a mother might develop an inseparable bond on seeing her newborn, and possibly even change her mind about the entire adoption process. So, for newborns about to be adopted, the procedure at the time was that mothers were not allowed to see their babies.

Within seconds of my birth, I was hidden from my own mother behind a curtain. I was taken away from her, denied those first few moments of being held by her or feeling the warmth of her cheek pressed against my skin.

After being wrapped up, out of her sight, I was taken into another room and placed in a crib. A hospital privacy curtain was drawn around my crib, cutting me off from any chance of being seen by the woman who'd just given birth to me.

I was isolated. And alone.

Growing up, I had never known this was what hospitals did with babies that were being adopted.

I began to wonder if being denied that hug and maternal connection during my first two days was connected in some way with my capacity in later years to detach myself from a group of people and analyze my surroundings, as if I were passively watching a movie.

Did this create my introverted view of life? Was this the source of my craving to feel liked? Or my fear of being abandoned and being isolated?

Deep in my thoughts, I would carry that isolated feeling. And I would carry it alone, sharing its existence with fewer than four people over the course of my life.

While my mother never saw me, my grandfather did, briefly, on the third day of my life. That morning he slowly picked me up, giving me that hug and comfort that I had been craving those first two days. He was so gentle. Having raised several children of his own, that paternal instinct kicked in as he held me close. He knew that in a short while, he'd be giving me up, and he wanted this memory to last.

The choices that had led up to this moment weighed on his shoulders like a heavy blanket as he helped his daughter carry out her wish to give me a life she couldn't provide. Did he still have time to change this course of action? He wondered if he would live out the rest of his life with guilt that he was the one who, in the end, actually handed me over to someone else?

How would Susan feel in the coming months or years? Would she lock this away deep inside and never want to talk about it again to anyone? He thought about the complex emotions that would resurface if, somehow, she and I were brought together again. How would such a reunion be affected by this choice right now?

As he thought about these things, he held me tightly in his arms. Slowly, he walked down the quiet hall to another room, to the mediator of the adoption. Then he reluctantly gave his first grandchild away.

That is when my grandfather became my only blood relative to hold me or see me.

When I learned about this, I realized he was the key to my story. Grampy was the last to hold me. And his name was the first I found when searching for my family in Bad Bob's family tree. It seemed appropriate that he was the one tying it all together.

For the next few years, my grandfather would hear whispers of his grandson's life through the conduit of the mutual friend through whom the adoption had been arranged. These random stories from my new life would comfort him for a few years.

But then two isolated events occurred that would sever that tie, end that comfort, and wipe out any chance that my grandfather would somehow keep me in his family's life.

First, the mutual friend passed away, which shut off the discreet flow of information to my birth family. He would never hear any more news of his grandson's soccer games or cub scouts.

Second, not long after this, my adoptive parents separated and my mom, brother and I moved away from Boston, to live in Lancaster to be closer to my mom's family.

In an age before the Internet, and with no one to relay this crucial bit of information, I had simply vanished off the face of the planet.

The Countdown

After vanishing without a trace from my biological family decades earlier, we had now found each other. The week of July 4th in 2018 was without a doubt extraordinary in every way that other weeks were not. I had found my birth mom and my aunt. I'd learned I had two sisters. And in a week and a half, I'd be on a plane flying to Florida to meet them.

As I drove through our parking lot at work that Wednesday morning, I gazed at the rolling farmland to the left of the theater and realized that in ten days I'd be looking instead at the rolling ocean waves of Palm Beach.

My excitement had been rising. I felt like a kid on Christmas Eve again, anticipating what the morning would bring. But this was much more remarkable. Something had been lacking, some mystery had been nagging at me my whole life, and now that I was on the verge of discovering what I had been missing, I felt the exhilaration building. This trip would be the culmination of years of searching.

I found I was thinking in new categories. For 43 years, my family had always simply been my family - my mom, my brother. I'd never thought of them as my adoptive family. But now I had this second family - or should I think of them as my first family, though we'd never met? Perhaps, I realized, it really didn't matter what I called them. I just wanted to meet them.

Despite this being a week unlike any I had previously experienced, I wanted to somehow add some normal back into the week.

So I posted a picture on social media.

A few minutes before I took the photo, I had written a large number one on an index card and a large number zero on another index card. Though I had learned to understand binary computer code in college, with all its 1s and 0s, the reason I had written these two specific numbers had nothing to do with binary. It did have something to do with the fact that in precisely ten days, I would be on a plane to meet my family.

For the record, the number "10" - in binary - is the number most people refer to as "2", which is exactly the number of times I had to take the picture of myself holding the numbers, because the first time I had the cards backwards and it read "01" which was not precisely how many days were left until my trip.

After taking the picture of myself holding the numbers with Lancaster farmland behind me, I opened the picture up in Photoshop and added the words "more days" after the number ten.

In the comment above the photo, I wrote that in "ten more days" I would be standing at a Florida beach instead of the farmland and would be with my family. I added the #countdown hashtag as a joke.

A few hours after posting that picture to social media, I received a text from Christina. My sister had taken a picture of herself holding a handwritten number ten along with a comment about looking forward to my coming down to see them.

Well that's interesting, I thought. Seems Christina and I share a similar sense of humor.

Later that night, this unofficial countdown became very official. Both Sarah and Christina sent a text message, along with a video. It was the two of them sitting in a car. In the background I could hear the song "The Final Countdown" playing.

"Hi Scott!" they both said together. "Guess what today is?" Then the two broke into song to the beat of the song, singing their rendition, "It's the Ten-Day Countdown!"

Oh that was gooooood, I thought to myself. They *are* like me.

If they were going to go to this level, I would have to pull from my years of experience performing as a comedy magician.

It's on, I thought. Oh. It was on.

※

The next morning, I enlisted the help of one of my coworkers to film me with my phone.

"Hey Scott, how many days until you visit your family?" he asked off-camera. As he pointed the phone's camera at me, I held up a deck of cards with the ten of clubs showing on the face of the deck.

"Well, yesterday it was ten days. But today, it's nine." I waved my hand over the ten of clubs and it visually changed into a nine of clubs. It was a simple magic trick that I had been doing for almost twenty years. Let's see what they think of that #*countdown*!

It worked.

"How? Just how?" Christina's text said to me moments later. Sarah's text quickly followed. "You. Win. Already. That was pretty cool, I'll give you that."

They loved it and wanted to know how I had done it. That kicked off a flurry of text messages between us for the rest of the day. These daily back-and-forth countdowns were letting us all have fun and get to know each other before we ever met in person. It was amazing.

We were not a few strangers awkwardly wondering what to talk about next. We were laughing and joking, having a hard time not talking.

I had given my wife a hard time for years about how much she would text people. How could she possibly text that often? Now, for the first time in my life, I found myself on the opposite side of that thought. I was having constant text conversations with my two sisters.

It. Was. Constant.

In one, Christina sent a photo of her two boys napping on the couch. "Look, I can do magic too!!" she said in the text. "Having these kids take a nap at the same time is almost impossible haha. Stay tuned for the 8 day countdown."

I felt a connection with them that was how I imagined it would be if I had known them for my entire life. That isolated feeling I'd had most of my life was absent during these weeks leading up to the trip. Was this absence of loneliness temporary? Was this bond I was building with my sisters something that wouldn't last? It was easy to text them. What were they like in person, though? Would our conversation continue to feel this natural?

I was thinking how much I'd love it if this bond developed even more, and I found someone who got me for being me. Someone like me.

Each day brought a new conversation, new things to talk about, and new pictures being exchanged. Sometimes we would text mundane things, about going to the gym, or running, or pepper plants. Other times, it was about much bigger things, such as Sarah getting ready to take her NCLEX nursing exam the next week.

On the eighth day before my trip, I received another countdown text. What did my sisters have in mind this time?

There was a video: Sarah and Christina, sitting with their kids. Sarah had her three next to Christina's two. Getting that many young kids to sit long enough for a video had to be a magic trick in itself, I thought. They were off to a good start.

Then, one by one, each of their kids raised their hands and shouted a number. One of them shouted "One!" Then next said, "Two!" Three. Four. Five, they continued. Christina smiled and announced loudly, "Six!" Sarah, grinning, said, "Seven!"

Then, out of the blue, my mom appeared from behind them, standing up from her hiding spot and said, "Eight more days!"

For. The. Win. They had trumped my magic trick. They had all pulled together for such a fun countdown.

I loved that my mom and sisters had come together as one family, for me. And seeing my mom at the end of the video was perfect. I could see she was having a lot of fun making the video with her two daughters, just for her son.

Ever since I'd begun this search, I had wondered what she would be like. Was she serious or easygoing? Was she more about proper appearances, or just carefree? This video was a chance for me to see her personality really come through. On the phone, we'd had great talks. But I was pleased to see in this video how much she still liked to have fun.

Plus, it wasn't just one or two from the family excited to see me. They were all in it together. We all were.

Throughout the next several days, we continued. Sometimes my countdowns were better, but mostly theirs were more creative. And we were all loving every minute of it.

One day, they got together and wrote a poem about their eagerness to see me, plus other things we had talked about. I loved it. Their last stanza captured exactly how I felt, too:

> *In just 7 days we will all meet,*
> *then our lives will finally be complete.*
> *But until then, before your plane lands on Florida ground,*
> *let's have fun with this countdown to make up for lost*
> *days on the playground.*

Four days before the trip, they made pancakes in the shape of a four. Christina sent a text after the pancake picture. "You better think of something really good to top our pancakes lol,"

"Syrup?" I replied.

"Of course.. and butter," she said back. I gave it a beat. Then another. Sure enough, she sent a second text. "Haha I just had a moment... I didn't realize your answer to 'top our pancakes' was ... syrup! Mention this to NO-ONE."

These little moments were fantastic, and I was loving every one of them. Angie had told me countless stories of how she and her three brothers would play jokes on each other and tease each other. It was like the four of them had always been playing together. I was a bit jealous because I never had that, growing up. My brother and I got along great, but we just never took it to that level, since we were each, more often than not, off with our own circle of friends.

Now I had two sisters that I was learning more about each day. My brother was five years younger than me. My sisters were even younger - Christina was 29 and Sarah, 31. Though I was twelve years older, we got along so naturally, telling stories about each other's lives as though we were reliving the shared childhood we never had.

We'd known each other only two weeks, and already we were starting to tease each other as though we had grown up together. Sometimes it was a tongue-in-cheek joke at the other's expense. Other times it was taking my sister's text message about not getting a pancake joke and being able to add it to a published book.

※

It was coming up on just a few days before my trip to Florida. I would be leaving early on a Friday morning. But this Wednesday, I had something in store for them.

As an animator and visual effects artist, I am able to do pretty much any type of special effect with video - even create animated camels.

It was settled in my mind. I walked over to the animal barn behind my office to film a quick video with my phone. Not long after, both of my sisters got a text from their brother.

"Hey! It's two more days until I fly down on Friday, which means, you know what today is? It's hump day!"

With that I turned my phone to the side slightly to reveal two camels just hanging out behind me. On the video, with the help of CGI magic, one of the two camels turns his head to face the camera, opens his mouth and casually says, "Two more days, sisters!"

Hump day was introduced with a talking camel.

"How in Tarnations?" they replied. "I just had to watch that 4 times."

There was no "One More Day" video. I think the camels had ended the #countdown. Instead, we resumed simply texting each other and talking about how, in one more day, we'd be meeting.

"Can't wait to finally meet you and Angie tomorrow. Try to get some sleep," Christina said to me the night before the flight. This was it. It was finally happening and none of us would be able to sleep.

Stepping out of the plane and feeling Florida's humid air, Angie and I gave at each other a knowing glance. *We are here. What a journey.* In just a short while, I would be meeting my mom, sisters, and aunt for the first time.

The final picture I sent was from a parking lot in Florida. We buckled up in the rental car and began our drive to my mom's house in Palm Beach from the Fort Lauderdale airport. On the way, we stopped at a convenience store to get a bottle of water.

"Angie, can I have that piece of paper?" I asked, motioning to a piece of scrap paper in her purse. She handed it to me and I quickly scribbled a big "0 days" on it, then took a picture of myself holding it. Seconds later I heard the swoosh sound as my phone sent it to Christina.

She sent a picture back almost immediately, making a zero with her hands, with a huge smile on her face. "Welcome to Florida!" she said in the next text.

The next time we talk, it will be face to face, I thought. Face. To. Face. I had seen all of their faces in the pictures we had been exchanging these past few weeks. But to be able to hug them and look them in the eyes: to be able to see my family for the first time - that moment was right around the corner. Literally.

We got back on the road and turned down one more street into a development. As we drove, I could see, between the palm trees and houses, the lake that my mom had mentioned was behind her back yard. The house numbers were getting close to hers.

In just a few moments my wife and I would be pulling into their driveway.

Reunion

Angie and I pulled into the driveway in our rental car.

There was a lot planned for that Friday, besides our arrival. Auntie Laura, my birth mom's sister, was also flying down from Boston to be here for the occasion. And to top it off, Sarah had, just weeks prior, graduated from nursing school and today was her NCLEX (National Council Licensure Exam). Passing this exam was the final requirement to become certified as a nurse.

The plan had been that my mother would drive to the airport and pick up Auntie Laura when her plane landed at Palm Beach International so they could both be at the house as we arrived later that morning. The airlines would have none of that storybook tale, however. For whatever reason, her plane was delayed slightly.

Since Angie and I had already landed and were en route to my birth mom's house, my sister went to pick up her aunt at the airport so her mom could be at the house when we arrived.

I could only assume Christina felt it would be more appropriate for her mom to be the first one to meet me. She was only 29, but had the kind of maturity that prompted my auntie to describe her, during a phone call with me, as an "old soul." So Christina volunteered to leave and pick up Auntie Laura instead, knowing she would now miss that first big moment.

My first hint about this change of plans was when I received the text photo from Christina in which she was responding to my "zero days left" text, making her own "zero" with her hands. But instead of sitting in a house waiting, she was standing in a parking garage, about to pick up her aunt at the airport.

After getting that text, I thought that sounded like something she would do. In all my talks with her, she was always thinking of others before herself. Always. This morning, it was a selfless sacrifice that she made so someone she loved could enjoy that moment.

When I realized she was at the airport, I knew I would still meet her. It would just be a little later in the day, and with Auntie Laura.

This will be a day of staggered meetings, I thought, reflecting on how everything was playing out. I already knew Sarah was going to miss the initial meeting and instead be stopping by later that evening after she finished taking her NCLEX exam.

After pulling into the driveway and putting the car in park, Angie and I got out and looked at each other for a moment.

This was it. My birth mother was in this house.

All morning, I had tried to imagine how I might feel at this moment, but it was impossible to know for sure. Would I get butterflies in my stomach? Would I be excited? Afraid?

When you're about to meet a celebrity, or a potential boss, or even a blind date, there is that heart-fluttering moment just before, when you wonder what will happen next. Will I say the right thing? Will I make a good impression? Will he or she like me?

But most of us never have that moment with our mothers. She's just always been there, always been Mom. She's the one who held us as a baby, taught us letters and words, guided us through adolescence, was there for graduations and weddings. It was that way with my adoptive mom. I loved her from the very beginning. She was and will always be, simply, Mom.

But for a small group of people, there comes a day when the door opens, literally and figuratively, to meeting the one who gave birth to us. That moment, for me, was now seconds away.

As we pulled in the driveway I feared I would be nervous. What happened was surprising. I felt a calm come over me. My heart wasn't racing like I thought it would. It could have been because we had spoken so often in the past two weeks that I was already comfortable and felt like I knew my birth family.

God had been there all along, giving me assurance and comfort. It was a feeling of a warm, heavy blanket draping over me that allowed me to step out of the car and walk towards her front door.

Somehow, while I felt an inner tranquility, it was fringed with an excitement bordering on giddiness.

"Angie, here take my phone," I said as she came around the car. "I want to record this so they can watch it from our side." I pulled my phone out of my pocket and Angie begin to record a video of me walking up to the door to meet my birth mother for the first time.

As I walked up to the door, Angie followed closely behind.

"I'm going to finally meet my mom!" I said as I turned back to look into the camera. Every few feet, I'd turn back again, look at her and smile, with that excited feeling. In a few steps I was about to meet my birth mother.

I was a few feet from the door when I saw it begin to open.

Immediately, I saw my birth mother step out through the door. It was her! Until this instant, I had only seen a few photos sent via text. But, now, my mom was right here, standing directly in front of me.

I didn't even say hello. I simply reached out and hugged her. For the first time in our lives, we hugged. We had both been denied that hug in the moments after I was born, when I was taken from her to another room under the adoption protocol. It had taken over four decades to just be able to just hold onto my mom. I briefly let go to stand back a moment and look at her again, then just hugged her once more.

There she was in person. Though I had seen her in the pictures we exchanged, and the videos we were sending back and forth, seeing my own mother in person for the first time was like meeting someone new that I had known forever. As she smiled, I caught her eyebrows rising in just the same mannerism that I had.

Never again would I have to wonder. Never again would I have to analyze an infinite number of possible outcomes as to how she would react. It was here. Now.

And it was, well, *comfortable.* That really is the most appropriate word. One of the fears I'd had was that we would meet and the time would be filled with an uncomfortable silence as we sat together awkwardly. But it was comfortable, as though we had known each other all along. Like being with my family back home.

For the first time, my mom could be with her son. She was 18 when she had said goodbye to me without even seeing my face. She was 61 now. A long time to miss her son.

"I couldn't believe it. I thought I had lost you forever and I'd never see you again. But you found us. My son is back," she told me later that day. "My whole life, you can't imagine that feeling that there is a piece of you missing. I never thought I would get that piece back."

As she was saying that, I looked at her face and saw more similarities: our eyes, the shape of our cheeks, the same dark hair.

There were still some unknowns. One thing my grandfather had said when we spoke was that, when he saw my photo, he thought I looked just like my father. Yet as I looked at my mother, I could see where I got many of my features. *What did I get from my father?* I wondered. He was still a mystery. Then there's personality. How much of my personality did I get from her? What about my father? Maybe she would be able to tell me about him as we sat down to talk later.

Eventually, I let go and she turned to give Angie a hug. I made my way into the house and was able to see inside. Then I noticed something: there was someone else inside. Someone I hadn't expected to be there.

With both hands held up to her mouth in sheer joy, her eyes already tearing, I saw my sister Sarah standing just inside the door, with her daughter, Brooke, both watching me embracing my mom for the first time.

What was Sarah doing here!? She was supposed to be taking her exam today. I immediately went toward her, about to ask, "What are you doing here?" But the words never came out. Before I could say anything, she reached out and hugged her brother.

"I was getting ready to leave for the test," she said. "Then mom got your text saying you were just a few blocks away. I had to meet you and get it out of the way so I wouldn't be thinking about it all day! You know how much that would distract me during the test!"

I did. Yes. She was definitely like me. I realized that, had the roles been reversed, I probably would have waited to go take the exam also. After all, how could I possibly take a test if I knew my long-lost sister was on her way? I'd never be able to concentrate. Was she as determined as me? It seemed, despite our twelve-year age difference, that she and I were very much alike.

Her light blue eyes, so closely resembling mine, were filled with tears, but also joy. I'm sure she saw the same thing in me. It was, indeed, joy.

It was also surreal.

Until now, my family had existed only in photos for me. And now, I was talking with my birth mother, my sister. We were the same flesh and blood. And we were together.

Once everyone was inside, Brooke came up to me with a giant smile on her face, gave me a hug, and introduced herself. My niece. She walked to me with a delicate, yet graceful motion that I was unaccustomed to seeing from a ten-year old. I could tell she was excited to meet me that day and tell me all about her many achievements.

"I'm a dancer. Would you like to see my routine?" she asked. Ah. That explained her grace in moving. She was in both dance and gymnastics, quite the overachiever.

Everyone was talking, laughing, hugging. Our conversations were a blur. We kept telling each other how we couldn't believe this was happening and this was going to be such an amazing weekend. But then, Sarah had to leave.

"Brother," Sarah said to me, with tears still in her eyes. I could see how happy she was to be able to call me that. "I'll be back. I'm so glad you're here. I have to go take that test now. I hope I pass."

"You'll do fine," I told her. I knew she was smart. She was going to pass. "We'll be here. Then tonight, we'll celebrate."

It would be a few hours, most likely. But after years of waiting we had finally met. Sarah gave me one more hug and then, just five minutes after we met, my sister left for her test.

After Sarah left, my mom opened a bottle of red wine and we sat down and started talking. We had 43 years of catching up to do! It was all so comfortable to talk with them, I thought to myself again. What was it that had allowed me to open up so easily with my birth family? I had done that with Angie years ago, but here I was, at almost that same comfort level, and I had only been with them face-to-face for minutes.

"So, how was your flight?" my mom asked us. "What did you want to do while you're in Palm Beach?"

We only had a few days. I hadn't made any concrete plans, since I had wanted to wait to see how today would go first. So far, today was good. Very good.

"Our flight was great. It was a smooth ride. Angie and I were talking on the flight about what to do, and we're okay with anything, really," I replied as I sipped my glass of cabernet sauvignon. While talking on the phone earlier in the week, I had mentioned my love of red wines. Christina told me she picked up some reds, even though she was more of a white wine drinker.

"Well I think Auntie Laura has a few things she was thinking of doing," my mom said. "We can go to the Intracoastal and grab a bite to eat, and you have to go to the beach. But today, I think once Auntie Laura and Christina get here, we'll relax and have a nice evening of talking, some wine, and cheese."

That's right! Auntie Laura and Christina would be here shortly. I didn't realize how fast the time had flown.

"They should be here any moment," my mom said. "You know she's been looking for you for some time? I first told her about you back in 2009. You should have heard her when I told her she had a brother!"

"Really? What was that like?" I asked.

Looking for my Brother

"I have a brother?" Christina responded with excitement to her mom's revelation. Until that Thanksgiving morning in 2009, the only sibling Christina had known was her older sister, Sarah.

The two sisters had grown up very close, and not just because they were born just two years apart. They were close in the way best friends become after spending a lifetime together. They would finish each other's sentences and spoke in a very similar way, and not just in manner. Their voices sounded almost identical—so much so that the two played telephone pranks while they were growing up. While on the phone, Sarah would secretly hand the receiver off to Christina, or vice versa, trying to fool the person on the other end.

But there was something missing in their life. Something sizable.

One summer, Sarah confided to a friend, "Even though my sister and I are close, we've always hoped for a third sibling. I don't think you can understand how much we always wanted a brother to be close with."

But they would grow up not knowing why they had that feeling. Just as I never knew if I had brothers or sisters, they never knew about me because their mother had made a promise to her husband, Mr. C.

Though he knew I had been born and given up for adoption years earlier, for many reasons, it was decided to keep this information from his side of the family. This also meant that when their daughters were born, they would grow up without knowing about me.

Susan hoped the day would come eventually when it would be possible for her to tell her daughters about what had happened years ago. She had no idea how she would explain it all. But she would tell them they had a brother. She'd tell them about the cruise ship, about giving her son up for adoption. And she would tell them everything she knew about their brother. Maybe. If that day ever came.

But for now, their two daughters would grow to adulthood not knowing that the brother they had hoped for was actually out there.

※

My mom, in contrast, had always been open about my adoption, though she had given me few details about it, beyond the fact my birth mother wasn't able to care for me. I rarely spoke about it in middle or high school, but I felt lucky and deeply loved to know that she had gone to such extraordinary efforts to bring me into her family. Her family never felt like my "second" family. It was the only family I knew, and I felt loved by her and everyone else in that family.

Yet, with this knowledge that I was adopted came something else. The mind of an analytic can be a dangerous place. The game of "what if" is always running, like a computer testing simulations to find the best outcome. Except, for me, most of the time my mind wasn't running simulations for an upcoming decision. It was reevaluating past decisions. Trying to analyze why something happened.

What would have happened if I had stayed in Boston instead of moving to Pennsylvania? What would have happened if I stayed in engineering instead of graphic design? The list of "what ifs" was endless.

What if I had another life? A secret life?

Sure, I had, like many kids, dreamed of what it would be like to live another life. Secret-agent level stuff. But there was a level to that question much closer to my heart.

For me, that question had much more significance because I did have another life. Unlike most people, unlike my friends, unlike everyone I knew, I was living that other life. My question wasn't about what it was like to live a new life. I wanted to know what my first life was like, before this second life.

There was always a hint of curiosity about my birth mother and what that other life would have been like. And with that thought came more questions.

Why was I given up? It was a question I grew up pondering, though I hid that from everyone I knew except a few very close friends. There were plenty of hypothetical scenarios: Was it because she was more interested in herself? Was it because of drugs? Was I taken from her? Did she know she couldn't give me something and she wanted me to be better off?

Or worse, was I, somehow, not what she wanted in a child? Was I a burden to her? And then I would feel guilt at times.

Did she want to find me? Did I cause some trauma for her? If I reached out, would she reject me because of that pain?

That thought scared me more than anything, in the deepest part of my soul. I already had those thoughts of detachment and isolation from those around me. What would happen if I learned that the person who gave me life gave me away so she would never have to deal with me again?

That would be the ultimate rejection and would leave me feeling truly isolated. If I was introverted already and internalizing my life as much as I was now, how much deeper would that push me into the abyss? I didn't want to think about that too much.

Growing up not knowing your sibling existed, like my sisters had, would at least offer the gift of a normal life without those thousands of questions I had shouting silently in my head for a lifetime.

But sometimes we are given information whether we are ready for it or not. I grew up not knowing why I was given up, nor that I had two sisters. My sisters were growing up not knowing I even existed. Yet somehow they still had that subconscious draw towards another sibling. And I had that urge to be connected to someone similar to me.

We were two ships sailing past each other in the fog, each oblivious of the other.

※

Extraordinary things sometimes happen to us right under our noses. Most of the time, we go about our lives unaware of why some people come into our life or leave it. One huge comfort from my study of the Bible was how God has a way of bringing people into each other's lives at just the right moment for his purpose. He is in control, which meant that I didn't have to worry or be anxious for what tomorrow would bring.

In the Old Testament, the book of Ruth, specifically, is filled with these examples. In the second chapter of Ruth, it says that Ruth went to gather grain and, "as it happened," ended up doing so in a field belonging to Boaz, whom she eventually married. There are many other "coincidences" in this book, which culminates in the birth of Ruth's son, who becomes the grandfather to King David, in the direct lineage of Jesus Christ. Proverbs 16:33 tells us that while something may look random, it is decided by God.

But that's a hard concept to accept when there is pain involved. There's a flip phrase we hear all too often: *Everything happens for a reason.* Tell that to a parent who just lost a child to cancer.

Humans hurt. Even if some good comes from something horrible, the suffering remains. On the other side of the coin, the existence of pain and suffering doesn't rule out that there might be a significant purpose to be found in it, even if that purpose isn't for us. We may hurt so another will be presented with something greater. The story at the center of the gospel suggests God did just this with Jesus dying on the cross. One man's suffering and pain led the way for God's adoption of us into his family.

Pain has levels. Sometimes the pain of a marital breakup is described as ripping the bandage off quickly. But it's a terrible analogy. The pain of a band-aid coming off can't compare to that of a partnership coming to an end. But I have come to believe that, when someone must sadly move out of someone else's life, it may be God's way of allowing them to help someone else, even if indirectly. And in doing so, he is using us for his purpose and glory. Mr. C eventually became that needed catalyst for an explosive revelation.

After many years of marriage, Mr. C and Susan eventually realized they were drifting apart and made the hard decision to separate. And when their marriage was dissolved, so too was that marital vow to keep my existence a secret.

Susan was finally free to tell her two grown daughters what their grandfather had known for decades. It took her a few months to build the courage to do so, but when they both stopped over on Thanksgiving, she decided to tell them. She had her girls, now 20 and 22, sit down on the bed in their old room.

"I have a brother!" Christina said again as it began to sink in.

My mom told her daughters all about what happened years ago. She told them of the cruise ship. Of the pain of giving up her son, and the pain of not being able to tell them for years about their brother. She told them my name, age and a few other bits of information she knew.

But one crucial bit of information was still missing. Like her grandfather and her mother, Christina didn't know that I had moved out of the Boston area to rural Pennsylvania. But from that day on, she had a new goal in life.

That day, she began looking for her brother. Searching for me.

※

In the spring of 2018, Christina was still contacting strangers who shared my name. The mathematician in me goes straight to thinking about the sheer odds against finding me this way, and the utter devastation of hearing so many rejections.

The English alphabet has 26 letters. Those letters can be combined to create a finite lexicon, and an even more finite list of English names. Considering that surnames don't change, and first names tend to follow rough popularity trends, the number of unique American names drops drastically. As a result, names get reused by different families, more often than we realize.

A quick search online recently found that there were at least 91 other people sharing my exact name right now - just within the city limits of Boston. Expand that out to the surrounding counties, the rest of Massachusetts, and finally the rest of the country, and the number quickly approaches the number of processed ingredients in a fast food burger.

Interestingly, one person with my name made his way into the national news. A few years ago a man with an identical name was convicted as part of a $3.8-billion accounting fraud scandal and dominated the national news for weeks. Yup. Nothing like hearing your name on the nightly news for weeks in connection with the largest accounting scandal in history. I still have to wonder if my mortgage application was affected by this.

Christina, little by little, went digging through those names, one by one, hoping one day to find a match for her sibling. And one by one, she had to strike a line through each name she contacted.

With each negative reply, her feeling of despair at ever finding her phantom brother grew. Then the second-guessing began. Did the person she just contact lie? Was it really him, but he denied being her brother because he didn't want to be found?

One sunny Friday afternoon, Christina and her best friend went to get lunch and a drink. As they sat on the upper deck of the restaurant overlooking the water, Christina confessed she couldn't contain that much despair by herself. Years of searching and years of being rejected, month after month, had taken its toll on her.

"That had to be him," she finally said. "I just know it. He doesn't want anything to do with us." Her friend saw Christina's eyes watering as she said these words. It was as if saying the words out loud was driving a knife through her heart. She picked up her large sunglasses and slid them on to hide the tears that were beginning to fill her eyes. For the time being, all her friend could do was hug her.

"He has to be out there," she assured her.

For a while, Christina was the only one looking. But eventually, several states away, I began digging into my background. And now, sitting in Florida, we were about to meet for the first time.

The Photo

Christina told me later how she had woken that Friday morning of our arrival feeling both excited and anxious. This was the day she was meeting her brother! Years of searching had finally come to an end. Standing at the arrivals gate at Palm Beach International Airport, she would pick up Auntie Laura soon and head back to her mom's house on the other side of Palm Beach. A group of people walked past from an arriving flight. Christina peered into the approaching crowd, but her auntie wasn't there.

I wonder what he's feeling today?, she was thinking. *I bet auntie is just as excited.* The next surge of arriving passengers came around the corner. Sure enough, there was Auntie Laura, with a distinct skip in her walk. She was just as excited!

They recounted to me later what they had talked about on their drive from the airport.

"You think he's at Mom's already?" Christina asked. It was still early in the day, traffic was light, and they were making good time. "I'm sure they are there, talking right now."

"Oh, he has to be," Auntie Laura told her niece.

The drive home flew by as they talked about meeting me. Christina turned left at the last light, then made a quick right into her mom's neighborhood. She knew this neighborhood like the back of her hand. There were long rows of palm trees along the road to the left, lining the lake. She made the last left turn, following the perimeter of the lake. Just a few more blocks.

She pulled into the driveway and put her black SUV into park, next to the rental car already parked there.

"Here we go. All these years. I'm finally about to meet my brother," Christina told Laura as they got out of the car.

As if to take in every bit of this moment, Christina walked along the front walkway to her mom's front door, something she'd done hundreds of times, slower than ever before. Today was different. Today *he* was inside. Auntie Laura had walked ahead and was already inside before she made it to the door.

Christina told me later about the many thoughts that were pouring through her head at that moment. But the loudest one, she said, was simply: *That's my older brother.*

※

My mom was finishing up describing Christina's search for me when we heard a car pull up.

As the front door opened, I saw Auntie Laura first. She came straight to me, greeting me with a huge hug and a kiss on the cheek.

"Scott! Oh it's so good to finally meet you! Howahyou?" she said energetically in her unmistakable Boston accent asking how I was.

"I'm so good," I answered. "I still can't believe these last couple weeks."

"Overwhelmed yet?"

"Not yet. It'll probably all hit me later though!"

Hearing her voice in person took me back to that first phone call just weeks earlier. She was as dynamic and spirited in person as she was on the phone. After a beat, she turned to give Angie a hug.

I turned back towards the door, expecting Christina to still be a few feet away. But by then she was only half a step from me, mid-stride, her arms opening to give me a hug.

My sister. Was right there.

I had missed a lifetime of teasing her, watching her get her driver's license, graduate, go to the prom, and get her first job. I had missed her wedding. But right now, none of that mattered. She was here. I was here.

I reached my arms out and grabbed my sister to give her a hug for the first time. I saw her brown eyes for only a moment as she took that last step towards me. And in them, I saw she was thinking the same thing I was: *Finally.*

For a moment, I didn't hear anything around me. We hugged each other so tightly, and I didn't want to let go. Later, we joked that we had hugged so hard we crushed each other's chest bones.

"Scott," she whispered as we embraced. "Brother." It was the first time she had ever called someone *brother* to their face. I heard the emotion in her voice as she said it.

"I'm here, sis," I said, not even realizing until the words came out of my mouth that I had called her *sis*. I had done so on the phone and texting so many times in the past week. But just that one word, said almost inaudibly, was like a secret handshake, the key to a club I had never been a part of. A club that until that moment had only counted two sisters now had a brother.

It was a moment that lasted an eternity, though it was over in a flash. Finally, we let go and I looked at Christina again. Our two ships, once sailing past each other in the fog, would from this moment forward be cruising together on the adventure of a lifetime.

※

After a few more tears of happiness, we all began to settle in for the evening. It was going to be a good one.

"You look just like your father," my mom said as we sat around talking. "He and I spent so much time together on the ship. But after I left the cruise and went home, we talked less and less."

I tried to picture her with this Italian. She told me his name and I wondered if it ever would be possible to track him down. No links had come up in my DNA search on my Italian side. *Did Italians not do DNA tests like Americans?*, I wondered. *Maybe they are just more private than us. Maybe the tests are more expensive over there.*

"He was about ten years older than me, and from northern Italy," she told us.

"Really? Isn't that crazy. Angie and I stayed in northern Italy two years ago and we just loved it up there. We visited Milan, Lake Como, and Bellagio. It is so beautiful up there. Isn't that weird how I was drawn to that area!"

"Wow. That could be!"

I had been so close. Was he still there? A decade older would mean he was around 70. Was he even still alive? Now I felt an urgency to find him.

But that would be another search for another day. Right now I was here, with her. I focused back to the here and now.

"I love the view you have out back," I told her.

Her porch opened up to the east with a lake view property. We all made our way outside to take in the view. Across the lake, I could see the silhouette of several palm trees reaching up above a row of houses. Their reflection in the still water glimmered against the sun. I could only imagine what a sunrise would look like over this lake.

"Come on you two,"Auntie Laura said to Christina and me, while we were still out on the back porch. "Let me get a picture of you both."

As she held up her phone to take the photograph of me with my sister, it occurred to me then that this was the first picture I would have with anyone from my biological family.

Christina and I stood next to each other, embracing, while making back-and-forth jokes as we had done during our countdown. As she snapped the picture, we were both laughing.

"You two look so happy," Auntie Laura said as she looked at the photo before handing us her phone.

The emotion in that picture captured everything I was feeling that day. It was a great, fun picture, and it was easy to see in it how comfortable we were with each other.

When I stared at it more closely, I saw on my face an expression that hadn't been there in a long time. I was *only* being happy. It may sound odd to say that I was *only* happy. I had been happy before. But in daily life I am a supreme multitasker, skilled at optimizing even my thinking time. The result is that I've always felt like a human computer, always running something in the background while apparently living in the foreground. Rarely in life was I simply in the moment. I was usually thinking about something else: Sometimes it was a problem at work that I was trying to let "simmer" until I found a solution. Sometimes it was thinking about a book I was reading. Sometimes I was simply analyzing my current situation.

But today, I was in the moment. I was not happy *and* thinking about a Greek verb I had been doing a word study on. I was not happy *and* meditating on Psalm 8. I was only, well, happy. That face in the picture was just me, having fun. I had let my guard down completely with Christina. She and I were just laughing, having a good time. Without trying, I was doing what Angie had done her entire life. Angie would simply be in the conversation.

Had I done it? Had Christina become the first person, besides Angie, to get me to just be me? Every time I look at this picture, I think of that and how I was able to just … *be.*

※

That isn't to say that I didn't do any internalizing that day, mind you. Sitting there later that Friday evening, I had a moment where I first truly understood how much today marked the beginning of something very different. Everything had changed, and I was just barely beginning to grasp the significance of it.

Meeting Sarah and my mom in those first few minutes definitely evoked tears of joy for me. It was a huge moment. But sometimes the size of something becomes more apparent with repetition.

When Auntie Laura had told me about my mom on the phone the day before Independence Day, it was amazing. But then to have her tell me of my sisters, and then my grandfather, then to hand the phone to him so I could speak with him - after all that, I was barely able to stand up. Saying I had the wind knocked out of me would be a poor way of describing the magnitude of her cumulative revelations. It was like being slingshotted into the air with giant bungee cords, then snatched midair by a passing jet, then pushed into the back of the seat as a set of onboard rocket engines took the jet supersonic. Yeah, okay, I get that it's a crazy illustration. I mean, giant bungee cords? But that's the level of progressive revelation I was dealing with on the phone that day.

Being in Florida, meeting everyone in such a staggered way, made that previous experience feel tiny by comparison. Enough to get me to realize I should probably sit down sooner rather than later. All day, the significance of it grew, like a chain reaction of fireworks, accelerating when I looked at Auntie Laura's photo of Christina and me.

But it was that evening, after Sarah returned from writing her exam, that my mind was close to going into an uncontrolled nuclear explosion.

It hit me the most when Sarah sat down with all of us: For the first time in her life, my mom had all three of her children in the same room with her. For the first time in our lives, we were all together. Just hours before, we had never met, and now, here we were, sipping wine and chatting, as a family.

I sat back, imagining an infinite collection of moments that had never happened with the three of us under one roof: Christmas mornings. Birthday parties. Fourth of July picnics. But finally, the three of us were in the same room together.

The impact of the day was sinking in as I processed this new reality. Yet, I didn't feel overwhelmed. In an odd way, it felt completely natural and comfortable, even though I realized I would look back on this as a pivotal day in my life.

Christina and I had talked the week before about many things, including our common enjoyment of a fine wine. I had mentioned my love of reds, specifically.

As she poured a cabernet into my glass, I waited to sip it. Rather than drinking red wine right away, it should be allowed to breathe by letting it sit a moment. Perhaps subconsciously, I also paused to breathe. I inhaled deeply and slowly, observing the multiple, simultaneous conversations going on around me. It felt ... peaceful.

I caught Christina watching me as I sat there, relaxed, letting my wine breathe.

At that moment, it felt as though we were inside each other's minds. A squint of the eyes we both made at the same time and then the tiniest smirk convinced me she knew exactly what I was thinking.

"Christina," I asked her later, "were you thinking the same thing I was?"

"It was a feeling of peace," she said, perfectly echoing my thoughts. "A feeling of relief. No more searching for my brother. From now on, it would be moments of us telling stories, laughing, joking and being there for each other."

It was a sense of belonging.

Then it hit me.

I had felt this before. That Christmas morning so many years ago, when I opened up the set of encyclopedias. My mom got it. She knew I would love those books. It was because I did belong in her family. Hmm. I'd have to circle back to that after I got back from Florida, when I had more time to ponder what that meant.

Dinner Party

While my cabernet sat on the coffee table, breathing, I reached for a small piece of goat cheese topped with raspberry. It had been a while since I'd been able to simply enjoy some pleasant conversation accompanied by wine and cheese. It was refreshing.

"So, tell me about Bad Bob," Auntie Laura suggested. I had mentioned him briefly during my phone calls with her and with my mom and sisters before the trip, but only tangentially.

The evocation of his name instantly brought back memories of the search for my family, his sense of humor, and even the family distilleries from the turn of the century.

"I just got my results back from the DNA site and saw his name at the top," I started telling her. "At first, it was a slow start since we didn't know where to look in the family tree. But the more we emailed back and forth, the closer we got."

Researching DNA sometimes isn't about finding someone but doing enough research to eliminate everyone else.

"The links in the family tree he made were there all along, in plain view. He and I just had to painstakingly eliminate all the other people in his chart," I said.

Eventually, we turned our attention to food. They asked what we liked and rattled off a few local places to eat near Palm Beach.

"Susan," my auntie said to her sister, "they'll love the Key Lime House."

"What's that?" I asked her.

"It's one of my favorite places to grab lunch. It's right down Lantana Drive, by the Intracoastal. One thing you'll learn about being down here is that everything is down Lantana or Jog," she answered, referring to the two main roads in town.

In a way, I loved that we were just talking about mundane things like where to eat. It was like any other slow Friday evening conversation, as though being here was just normal.

But eventually we circled back to some extraordinary moments in our lives as my mom reminisced about the cruise, my birth and adoption.

"He was so much fun to be around," she started off, talking about my birth father, Mr F. "And I can see so many of his features in you. Your eyebrows are identical, and your smile. You have his smile."

I watched her focus shift from my face to somewhere off to the right and into the distance, as she thought back to the cruise over four decades ago.

Again, I tried to picture what he looked like. He was now the remaining piece of the puzzle of my birth and the question of who I was. She had no pictures of him and hadn't spoken to him since that year. Part of me wished so much she had at least one picture to share.

Later, when I spoke to my grandfather, he would reiterate how much I looked like my father. Earlier in the day, I recognized many of my mother's traits in me. But I would have to rely on my imagination to conjure a face that was me, yet wasn't.

"We tried to keep in touch, but it was so hard," my mother recalled. "We didn't have cell phones back then and could only call when his ship was in port. As much as we tried to keep in touch, we eventually talked less and less. It was so tough, because I hid the fact that I was pregnant from everyone for months. When I couldn't hide it any more from my father, I had to decide what to do. Over summer, I thought the only option I really had was to give you up for adoption. After I made this decision, I waited until the next time your father's cruise ship was in port. When he called, I told him I was pregnant and that I was giving you up for adoption."

She didn't elaborate on his reaction, and I didn't ask. I felt she and I would talk about it in more detail at another time.

There have been only a handful of times in my life where I felt so drawn into a person's story that I could literally feel their heartbreak or joy. Usually that came during a pause in the conversation, when I just looked deeply into the other person's eyes and saw in them the true sadness or joy that was in their heart. Such moments of connection may be fleeting, but they can feel like an eternity.

As my mom talked, holding a glass of wine in one hand, she was looking at Angie. I could see her reflecting back to those months when she had to make the choice of whether to raise a son as a single mother or give him up for adoption. Keeping me would mean sacrifices for both of us. She would have to work harder to support a growing son. I would miss out by not having both a mother and father, and most likely not be able to do many of the fun things kids do growing up. Giving me up, she knew, meant that her sacrifice would make it more likely that I could have a good life, never lacking the opportunities a complete family could give me.

In that instant I could see her pain, a pain that hadn't left her after a few months. It was a pain she still carried.

It would have been easier for her, I think, if she had known how well I was doing in my life. Knowing I had been given the motivation and support to receive my Eagle Scout Award. Knowing I had been given the chance to go to an exclusive private university. Knowing that I had the opportunity to pursue a career I wanted and not be stuck in a job I would hate.

Instead, she had made that sacrifice without the luxury of ever knowing if her sacrifice had made a difference for me. Never knowing if I had that better life that she wanted me to have. Always wondering in the back of her mind if her sacrifice had paid off.

"I had such a good life," I reassured her. "I got to do so many things growing up." I reflected on the many stories I'd heard of people who were abused growing up, or had lived with people with drug addictions in their home. "I never had any of that."

As I told her about the love I had been given, growing up, I saw two things in her eyes. The first was relief: she told me later how relieved she was to know now that I'd had those opportunities and been surrounded by a loving family. But under that relieved look was something harder to see. I caught a brief moment of anguish as she wondered if she had made a mistake and maybe could have given me that same life without the need for such a heavy sacrifice.

As quickly as I saw that look, it vanished. *The past is done,* she confided to me later. After all, here we were. We were all sitting here talking, eating, and laughing. It may have taken 43 years, but here we were.

That it did take 43 years for me to arrive in that seat with my mom and sisters does periodically make me wish I had begun my search sooner. But how would it have changed things? Would it have been better if I had searched sooner instead of waiting for so much time to pass?

※

In making wine, timing is crucial. Denying a wine the time to age properly can rob it of its maturity and give it a subpar taste.

Only God is able to fully understand why he guides us into each other's lives at specific moments. To question his reasoning, as the apostle Paul wrote in the ninth chapter of his letter to the Romans, would be like the clay pot questioning the potter, "Why did you make me like this?"

It took me most of my twenties and into my thirties to realize how much I was questioning the potter. At that point in my life, I thought I knew better than God. So I ridiculed him publicly and bragged about how I would have made a better-designed piece of pottery. Heck, I still do at times.

Had I been granted a taste for wine at that age, I likely would have bragged in ignorance how I could age wine in hours instead of months or years.

God graciously and patiently took my hand and allowed me to be distracted by my own self-interest until I had matured enough to be ready, before granting me a desire to seek my family. I've asked the question about why he allows things to happen or not happen many times in my life, and I have come to understand, albeit with only the wisdom of an infant, a possible reason.

Paul wrote in the opening to his letter to the church in Ephesus that God is *"working all things according to the purpose of his will."* (Ephesians 1:11, personally translated from the Byzantine Greek Text). While there are debates within Christian circles about the paradox between our free will and the will of God, one thing is expressed throughout scripture, which is that everything transpires "according to the purpose of his will."

It's still a mystery to me. If the greatest minds of the past two millennia haven't been able to come to a consensus, how do I stand a chance, except by his grace? Until the day that the answer is revealed, I confess I don't understand how we have free will, while everything is simultaneously under God's control and happens according to the purpose of his will.

Regardless of whether I fully grasped the reasons, when God was ready, and according to the timing of his plan, I was pulled from the darkness of my figurative wine cellar and allowed to breathe like the cabernet Christina had just poured for me.

My mother, my sisters, and I had all been given that time to prepare ourselves for this.

It was by God's grace that everything happened the way it did, and I trust it was because of his timing and planning for this reunion that our bond was so strong right from the beginning. Had I reached out years earlier, my own arrogance would have made for a bitter wine. I wanted to trust his timing, but in my lingering regret at not having started sooner on the search, there was still a hint of my arrogant *I know better than the potter* attitude. When I verbalized my disappointment about waiting to seek her, my mom knew better than to question the potter.

"This entire day has been incredible. It really makes me wish I started searching long ago," I lamented.

"It's all according to his plan," she responded. That phrase can easily sound cliché because it's said so often. But she was right. It is written in many places throughout scripture: Ephesians, Romans, even the often misused quote from Jeremiah 29 about God having plans of prosperity for us. Despite growing up over a thousand miles apart, my biological family and I had the same faith, and we all still trusted in this truth. His will and timing are perfect.

Even today, I feel I received a rare gift. I know of many others who are not welcomed into their birth families and it breaks my heart. But I am reassured by scripture that God is allowing something special to happen through that. Perhaps he is allowing someone time to breathe before building a relationship. We can only trust his wisdom.

She continued, "Your Grampy trusted in God's timing, and I see it, too."

Her father had an incredible faith in Christ, as I had learned while talking on the phone with him in our talks over the past couple of weeks. He and I spoke at great length about my recent trip to Israel. That trip had been life-changing for me and gave me a new sense of trust in God. That trust came from being there, where Jesus walked, and touching the actual history that had been only stories to me before that.

"What was it like there?" he had asked me the week before on the phone. "I wish I had gone there when I was younger."

"In one way," I began, "being able to go inside and touch Jesus Christ's tomb at the Church of the Holy Sepulcher, and kneeling down to touch the very spot where He was crucified several yards away, made it all so much more real. It was now tactile. But at the same time, when I was kneeling in Christ's tomb, I felt something else. Even though he was physically there in that tomb two thousand years ago, he was no longer there. He is now in us."

My Grampy also instilled that trust in God in his kids. One of his sons, my uncle, had become a pastor. We had taken different paths, but we still had been given that faith in Christ to trust him and his timing.

Because of his timing, my mom was sitting in her living room, enjoying a good wine, company, and laughs with all three of her children for the first time in her life.

※

I had spent only a few hours with them, but I was already feeling an unbreakable bond connecting us. I craved more of what I had experienced earlier with the photo, of just being in the moment. I felt this weekend would be a catalyst for more of those moments.

But as the evening came to a close, the old Scott resurfaced briefly. I remembered my good friend from high school, Diane, who had been abandoned on a porch as an infant. She had finally met her biological family a year before I found mine. She discovered a brother and several sisters living in the neighboring states. She remains close to many, but sadly, after a brief call, one sister won't return any calls. I know of another friend who, after finding his biological family, was told to never contact them again.

Would the next day and a half confirm the bond I'd felt forming during the dinner party, or reveal that it was all just surface-level pleasantries, and that after this weekend, we'd rarely, if ever, speak again?

The Ring Toss

While the countdown to my visit had pretty much solidified my belief that I was going to enjoy the company of my family once we met in Florida, I'd always known there was the chance that it could all flop and we'd end up sitting around staring awkwardly at each other. Friday had gone well, and we all had a great time. But one good day didn't mean things would continue that way.

The next morning, I was up before anyone else. I'm an early riser, and today was no different. I made a cup of coffee and quietly snuck outside to the porch overlooking the water. Such moments of solitude are peaceful for me. This is my time. The dawn began to paint the sky in beautiful reds and oranges, against the few clouds near the horizon. About halfway through my coffee, it was already beginning to rise above the horizon and hit the tops of some houses.

Watching this slow transformation of the sky, observing the reflections of the dark palm tree silhouettes on the far side of the lake, and listening to the faint lapping sound at the water's edge took me back to those several days I had spent at the shore of the Sea of Galilee in Israel. I was reminded of the renewed energy and calm state of mind I had experienced while sitting with my feet in the water of Galilee, reading scripture.

Just as it had been in Israel, this view and time helped my mind unwind and renew. It was my fresh start for the day.

This particular morning, as I was reflecting on the previous day, the old Scott wondered how things would go, now that we had gotten through our initial greetings. Would we simply run out of steam and be sick of each other by nightfall?

I was torn. On one hand, I wanted nothing more than to sit and talk. We had so much to catch up on. But on the other hand, I wanted to go do things with them. Create memories that we could remember for years to come.

As everyone started waking up and joining me outside, we began talking about what to do today. One thing was certain: Auntie Laura loved coming up with creative ideas for entertaining family. She had her favorite restaurants. She loved seeking new adventures, whether it was stand-up paddle boarding or eating sushi on the boardwalk.

These are what memories are made of. I was sold. I mean, what could go wrong? I was in Florida. At the beach. With my newly found family. It's not like I'd be swimming with sharks, right?

So I gladly followed her lead when she recommended a spot for Saturday's luncheon gathering.

Palm Beach consists of, well, a beach, and the rest of the city. And just to keep the beach from escaping, it is protected by a moat. The residents call this moat the Intracoastal Waterway, which is clever. Because it's a waterway, that's, well, between the beach and mainland. Think of it as something like an interstate, but made of water. And with fewer cars.

The Intracoastal runs parallel to, and is walking distance from, the beach. This is nice because if you get tired of the beach, you can walk to the Intracoastal Waterway. You'll be greeted by this big waterway, but since it's not really made for floating in unless you're a boat, you'll be forced to turn back to the beach unless you happen upon a bridge. There are a handful of these bridges, so you are lucky. Unless you're a boat. In that case, you most likely would prefer to take the waterway, not the bridge.

One of these bridges has a popular restaurant near it, called the Key Lime House. In addition to being right near the bridge, this popular restaurant also sits right on the waterway, which makes a pleasant view for those sitting out on the deck. It also happened to be where Auntie Laura wanted to take us for lunch.

She loved it here and made it a point to visit it with her sister as often as she could. I could see why. The view and atmosphere were fantastic: sailboats lined up along the docks, a gentle breeze along the Intracoastal, and a fun vibe at the restaurant.

Somehow, whether by accident or subtle collusion by everyone else, I ended up sitting near the center of a longer table. This placed me close to, well, everyone.

Since everybody else at the table already knew each other, Angie and I were bound to be the subject of the conversation. I also wanted to give my attention to everyone equally and not accidentally ignore anyone.

Sitting at the center of the table, I knew I'd be talking more than eating at this meal.

Growing up, I always seemed to find myself being good at things, but careful not to be too good. I was never the fastest runner on my cross-country team. I was consistently about the third fastest. Good enough to be better than average without being first, without drawing attention to myself.

I felt at times I did the same with my friends. I'd let them drive most conversations. It was more natural for me to sit back, watch, and analyze people. I'd listen to them and everything going on around us from that detached viewpoint. I could be a part of some great conversations without actually being the center of attention.

In a strange way, by placing myself close to but not quite at the top, I was able to surround myself with people who also strove for excellence and pushed themselves. I could learn from them while insulating myself from the fear of being overtaken scholastically, emotionally, or physically.

On an emotional level, I was far enough removed from them that I could observe without being observed. In my soul, I was afraid of being abandoned again, and this insulated me from being left behind.

But at the same time, that detached perspective meant I would never be alone, yet always alone, deep down.

When I found myself in this seat at the center of the table, I knew I wouldn't have the luxury of just listening to the conversation. I was the conversation.

While I was heavily engaged in laughing and talking with Auntie Laura and my mom, I caught myself observing a different conversation. Though my sisters and Angie were just at the edge of my peripheral vision, I knew they were talking about me. I could feel them staring at me as I talked to the others to my right. I could feel them pointing at something I did.

Turns out, as I learned later in the conversation, they were talking about how much I looked like and moved like their uncle. No. *Our uncle.*

Words have an incredible power to shape one's thinking. I was noticing that as I shifted from saying "your uncle" to "our uncle," there was no pushback. In fact, quite the opposite. They were doing the same thing, though I didn't catch it until a few minutes later. They had said that I reminded them of our uncle.

Once I caught my sisters saying that, I noticed it wasn't just them; everyone at the table had been doing the same thing.

I realized then that I wasn't just a stranger they would choose to ignore after I left this weekend. They had already accepted me as family, and subconsciously they were projecting this love and acceptance on me. It was a warm and inviting attitude.

I was also getting used to what at first was a novel experience: being told how similar I was to someone else in the family. Growing up, I knew without a doubt that I was loved by my family. But no one ever said how much I looked like a relative. "You have Grampy's eyes" was the kind of thing I had never heard before. But now everyone was saying it. Auntie Laura shared pictures of her sons, who shared certain features with me, too. Her oldest was even a programmer. And a photographer. *Well that's kinda like me,* I thought.

I began to think to myself: Okay, so we've got similar looks. But what about personalities? What did everyone do for fun when not entertaining long-lost relatives? Almost as if she'd heard my thoughts, Christina stood up and motioned to me.

"Follow me," she said, as she got up and started walking to the other side of the deck. "I want to show you something."

"Oh?"

"Trust me."

As we got to the other side, I saw a metal ring about three inches in diameter hanging from a fishing line about waist-high, like a giant pendulum, from a large wooden crossbeam above us. On another post, about twenty feet away, was a hook.

"It's called the Ring Toss. First one to land the ring onto the hook wins bragging rights," Christina said.

It was on.

She went first, to show how to first lift the ring, then drop it, letting it swing across the wide distance. On her first try, the ring came within an inch of slipping onto the hook. Yeah.

"You've done this before," I said to her, with a mock scowl on my face.

"Maybe. Your turn."

She watched as I stepped up to the painted line on the deck, being careful not to step over it, and pulled back on the ring, feeling its weight. I let it go and watched it swing towards the hook. Not only did it not even go far enough, but I was off to the side by a foot. I had to step up my game.

We continued for a few rounds of this, with neither one of us catching the hook. Finally, I realized that to hook it on, I had to hit the hook at an angle. So, as I released the ring, I gave it an ever-so-slight flick with my wrist. It went swinging across again, but this time, spinning in from the knot on the fishing line in a wide arc. It grazed the hook on the way up, and as it came back down, it slipped right onto the hook with a clang.

For a brief moment, I was thrilled. I won. But as we walked back to the table to join the others, I realized that was probably part of Christina's plan. She had played this game before. She knew the trick to hook the ring. *She had let her brother win,* I thought to myself. *Well played, sis.*

Regardless of who had hooked the ring first, I knew that we both won. After all, it was all about having fun. Just being with family and being ourselves. During the game, we'd had a great talk, off on our own. It was the first time she and I had

had the chance to be alone as two siblings. While we had talked so much in the weeks before this trip, that time just being with my sister, playing the Ring Toss, made me realize we would be close for the rest of our lives. There was never an awkward moment or forced conversation. Never a moment of second-guessing my decision to make this trip.

After lunch, everyone decided to walk to the beach. It was walking distance, and how can you go to West Palm Beach and not see the beach, right?

As we walked over the bridge, across the Intracoastal, my sisters and I were ahead of the rest of the group, talking and joking together. The fresh breeze coming from the shore was noticeable at the crest of the bridge. Below us, boats sailed along the Intracoastal. Through the steady noise of bridge traffic and the breeze, we heard Auntie Laura call, asking us to stop. She wanted a photo of us together. So my sisters and I stood next to each other in a group hug, against a backdrop of blue sky and waterway, and smiled as she took the first picture of all three siblings together.

While I stood there next to both of my sisters, I thought back to the past week and our exchanges. The countdown fun had shown that, even a thousand miles apart, we could have a blast with each other. And now that we were together, whether with a game of Ring Toss or just great conversation and laughter, we were going to have fun together. This sense of belonging I had so long hoped for was starting to come together. At the same time, I was beginning to understand that there was something here that tied in with my adoptive mom's love for me.

My analytical mind was starting up again. But this time, it was different. It was as though I was beginning to see the world in color for the first time. All the pieces of a lifetime were starting to align. I just wasn't sure how, yet.

Swimming With The Sharks

When I went to the beach as a kid in Boston, the water was frigid. In New Jersey, while the water was much warmer, it also dropped off from ankle-deep to chest-deep in a matter of steps. Additionally, the waves were pretty rough, with powerful undertows.

If you came to peacefully float around in serene, crystal clear water, you would soon realize that the feeling you were actually feeling was you being tossed around like a rag doll in a violent undertow.

If the *Jersey Undertow* was like eating red peppers and wasabi while being spun around with your eyes closed, the beach at Palm Beach and Delray was like sitting, drinking a relaxing green tea on a cool spring afternoon. The two were night and day.

On the beach, we laid out our towels on the sand. This was pretty much a necessity here. While New Jersey had some hot sand, Palm Beach sand, in August, felt like it was trying to form glass.

The ocean breeze, seagulls over the grass-covered dunes, and the calm waters reminded me of the rolling farmland in the photo I'd taken a week and a half ago. Here I was, in a wholly different world. The old me kicked in, wanting to resist just sitting at the beach. After all, the ocean is right here, I thought. I stood up and motioned towards the water.

"Let's go see how the water is," I said.

Sarah looked at me oddly. I figured she was just bored with the ocean, having spent her life with this beach just a few miles from her house. Finally, she stopped looking at me oddly.

"I'm alright," she answered before resuming her odd look at me.

I persisted.

Besides, I thought, Christina and I had had our time bonding during the Ring Toss back at the Key Lime House and I wanted to spend some time with Sarah doing the same. She stood up, reluctantly. I remembered her mentioning in one of our chats the week before that she was on the swim team when she was still in school. So I knew she wasn't being reluctant because she didn't know how to swim.

Regardless, she was following me into the water. Whatever the reason for her hesitation, either it wasn't that bad, or she was willing to deal with it so she could continue chatting and getting to know her brother.

The water was clear enough to see the tiny fish swimming all around us in the waist deep water. Once out deep enough to tread water, I looked back at the shore. There were really not many crashing waves. The waves at the beach were small and calm.

"The water has a gentle rolling motion that I really like," I said to her. "I love how relaxing and gentle the water is out here."

"It's like that because of the sandbars," Sarah told me.

"That makes sense." We'd had sandbars up in Daytona that made the same gentle, rolling waves my college buddies and I had loved. There was something else about the sandbars but I couldn't think of it right then. Was it the way the waves moved? Sigh. Analytical Scott was back as I tried to remember.

Then, in the blink of an eye, the moment of pure relaxation was lost. A chill went down my body. *The water isn't cold*, I thought. Quite the opposite. It was the perfect temperature.

My analytical mode had crept up quickly. Below the surface was some predatory thought that was chasing me away from having a good time. Was I afraid of something? What was it?

"I'm heading back in," Sarah said. We'd only been out there for about ten minutes or so before she began making her way back to the shore. Swiftly, too. I made sure to leave my analytical mode out there in the water as I followed her back to the others.

The August afternoon sun continued heating the sand. I think we had fully dried off before we even got back to the towels, it was that hot. It was the type of hot that makes one want to promptly leave the beach and grab some cold drinks, which we did.

As we were leaving, I realized I was no longer that kid playing Indiana Jones on the beach. I was no longer that kid spending my time wondering what everyone's fascination was with sitting on the beach on a towel. I didn't see it as a kid, but it made much more sense now. How had I missed something so simple all those years ago? Sure, the ocean was appealing, but it wasn't really about the beach. It was about the time with family.

Maybe I was learning to leave those analytical or predatory thoughts out there in the ocean, symbolically washing them away, so I could enjoy being in the moment more. Was I being too metaphorical?

※

"I know a great place to eat right across the street," Auntie Laura said as we painfully made our way across the burning sand, back to the road to wash off our feet with some refreshingly cold water and put our shoes back on. "*Boston's* is my favorite restaurant in Delray, and it's just a block down the street."

"*Boston's?* For real?" I asked. What are the chances, right? The Bostonian flies over a thousand miles to south Florida to eat at a place called *Boston's on the Beach.* How cool. I rolled with it.

When we got there, the deck was full, forcing us to go to their upstairs seating. I didn't mind today. We were seated against a window overlooking the beach and, even better, it was air-conditioned inside! I could definitely go for some cool air after the fire sand.

It was while we were sitting there that I witnessed something quite disturbing.

By pure coincidence, the 98 beats per minute logged permanently in my smartwatch while talking with Auntie Laura on the phone two weeks earlier was the exact heart rate I reached in the next few moments.

The moment was centered around a large tarpon jumping out of the water. This by itself isn't very disturbing. What made this jumping tarpon disturbing was that just behind the big fish, prompting it to jump out of the water, was a hammerhead shark. This sight obviously started a panic as people rushed to get out of the water. One person on the beach was making a video of it, which we discovered the next day had been uploaded to social media, allowing us to relive this disturbing event over and over. The joy. Upon realizing what was happening during the moment, though, my heart rate raced again to 98 beats per minute, a number stored forever in my smartphone's heart rate log.

Oh, how modern technology allows us to be able to retrieve this information.

Somehow, I had repeated my history. And not just with the same 98 beats per minute. I remembered instantly. The sandbar. Daytona. I turned pale. Just half an hour earlier, I had persuaded my reluctant sister into this same water to swim, telling her how the water was fine. Except this time it wasn't.

For the second time in my life I had been swimming with the sharks. And worse, after only meeting her the day before, I had almost caused my sister to be lunch for a shark.

Somehow, my predatory thoughts chasing me away from having a good time had manifested itself as an actual shark. For. Real.

"That sort of thing only happens in the movies," I said under my breath.

"What?" Sarah asked. "Sharks? No they are pretty common. Especially down here. That's why I don't like going in the water."

Checkmate, sister.

Metaphor or not, I now had a visual image of what was going on in my head. I was actively chasing away good times with my own predatory thoughts.

✳

The next day we would stay away from any sharks. Sunday there would be about ten of us at Christina's house for the party. This was the day Sarah would get her nursing exam results back. It would be either a pass or fail. And to start working as a nurse, she needed the certification from this exam to be officially licensed.

I knew she would pass. So did everyone else that afternoon. Still, Sarah was a bit nervous, what with her career riding on this one test. She had every right to be anxious. Truth be told, I would have been a wreck if I were in her place.

Most nurses who take the test are told they will receive the results of the test about forty-eight hours after they complete it. Her husband had taken it the year before and received the notice that he had passed two days later, to the hour. Still, it was a guess when the server would send Sarah's pass/fail notification.

So she sat. Waiting. Her eyes glued on her smartphone, swiping down on the digital screen to refresh. Everyone else was laughing, playing with the kids, and chatting with each other. I was, too, but I was also watching Sarah watching her phone. To lighten her mood, I sent her a text as I sat a few feet away from her.

"Stop hitting refresh, sis. You got this." She looked up at me from across the room, smiled, then put her phone down. Briefly.

During one moment between all the laughter, wine, and conversation, I caught Sarah's glance. I could see her mind working behind her eyes. She was analyzing her answers from Friday. Fully sure of herself, yet second-guessing. I was seeing many similarities with myself. She analyzed everything.

Seeing one of my traits in someone else was slightly jarring. It was like I was seeing my personality coming from someone else. *My sister shouldn't be analyzing like this right now,* I thought. *She should just be enjoying the afternoon, knowing she likely passed. She's smart. She knew the topics she got on the test were ones that she knew cold.*

Wait.

Was I just analyzing myself analyzing my sister's analyzing nature? I was falling down some rabbit hole. Here I was, around my family, people who were very much like me. And yet, I was still analyzing. For almost this entire trip, I had hardly done that at all. I had let my guard down with them to the point that I felt so comfortable talking with them. It felt good. So why all of a sudden did I lapse back into that other nature?

I pushed it away for now, figuring I could think about it later. I'd have to. My thoughts were interrupted by Sarah's phone. It had just buzzed on the counter. She had received an email.

Sarah stared at her phone on the counter. We all heard the distinct smartphone vibration and that instant, the room went silent. All eyes were on her. What would it say?

She picked up her phone, swiping across to unlock it.

While I had missed out on her recent graduation, being here for this moment helped me feel like a part of the family. As I looked around the room, I could see how close they all were. And I was in that room with them at this crucial moment, when just a few weeks ago we didn't even know each other. How fast things can change. And now it was Sarah's life that was about to change. In a moment, we would either be celebrating with or consoling her.

She tapped the blue mail icon, which had one new message showing. I watched her eyes scan the email. As they darted back and forth, reading the glowing screen of her phone, Sarah's eyes watered. *This is taking way too long,* I thought to myself.

She looked up and said, "I passed."

The room erupted in cheers. One by one everyone gave her a hug. Her eyes were visibly watering, as were mine. We were all so happy she had passed. Today was the beginning of her new career. I was thrilled to have had the privilege to be here for this important moment.

It's hard to recollect the rest of the party. Immediately after her announcement, we did a round of Fireball shots. It was time to celebrate. The rest was a blur. More congratulations, hugs, and tears.

The only part of the room not celebrating was a subcommittee of neurons having a meeting in my brain. They had decided to avoid the celebration in the rest of my brain and instead, went off into a dark corner to analyze why I had gone from fully open with my family to analyzing my sister for that brief moment.

I had found an unbreakable bond with them. Already, Christina and I were able to have long conversations with each other with just a glance, without even saying a word. Still, it felt like there was one piece to this puzzle that was missing. *What was it?*

The Return

As I stood by the sliding glass patio door overlooking the lake that Monday morning, I took in my last sunrise of the trip. Inside, the smell of bacon filled the air as we all helped ourselves to breakfast.

"Friday seems like ages ago," I said to my mom.

"I know," she replied. "Thank you for coming down. This was wonderful, having you here. We are all so thankful that you found us."

It had been wonderful, I thought. *But man did the weekend fly by.*

"I can't believe you have to leave already," Auntie Laura said. She was leaving in another day but was up early for breakfast and to see us off. "We'll see you again in a few weeks! It will be here before we know it!"

Auntie Laura had already decided earlier in the week that Angie and I would visit her in Boston. A giant family reunion was in the works with all my uncles and cousins. Christina, her husband and kids, would all pile in a car with our mom and drive north from Florida for it, too. I was looking forward to meeting the rest of the family, especially Grampy. There would be so many more laughs on that trip.

But for now, the morning was filled with hugs and tears. Except for the first day of my life, I had spent only three days with my birth family. Ever. And yet, in these past three days we had grown so close and experienced so much. It was something I would remember forever, no matter what happened in the future.

Meeting my biological mom. *My mom!* Being there for Sarah's nursing certification. Being able to bond so well with Christina. This was a weekend that would be tough to beat.

On the flight home, and for several weeks following, I began to analyze again. Only this time I was analyzing myself even more. What was different about them that allowed me to bond so well? Why was I so comfortable around them?

※

It was an extraordinary weekend, but life would quickly return to normal. The first sign that things were back to routine was an enthusiastic greeting from Dad.

One benefit of living where we did in Pennsylvania was that Angie and I lived close to several family members, Mom included, who could help watch my dad while we were away in Florida. Dad knew them, but I could tell he had missed us. She and I saw it when his face lit up with joy when we got back.

Angie and I were starving by the time we got home and we knew Dad would be hungry that late in the afternoon. We put some pasta to boil on the stove. As I looked at it cooking in the water, I wondered about Italy.

"You think we'll find him?" I asked her. My biological dad was over there, in Italy. Somewhere. My wife and I had both been there several times. But Italy still held a mystery for me. Who was he? Would I be going through all of this searching again? Could I expect the same warm reception and bonding I had in Florida?

"Maybe we'll have to plan another trip over there to look." I knew she wanted to go back to Italy. So did I. Now we had even more of a reason.

As I tried to imagine what my biological father was like, my adoptive dad put his crossword puzzle down on the kitchen table and looked up at me. He was getting fewer of the crossword answers these days due to his dementia's progression, but I figured it was good for him to keep trying, to keep his mind thinking and minimize the effects of the disease. So I struck up a conversation with him.

"It's great to be back from Florida, to be home again," I said to him.

"Oh, what did you two go to Florida for?" he asked me.

"We went to meet my biological mom and my two sisters."

"Did you have a fun trip with Karen?" he asked us. He had thought we went on a vacation to Florida with his ex-wife, my adoptive mom, Karen. I gave Angie a glance and she understood.

"Oh, Dad no, it was just Angie and me. We went to Florida to meet my biological mom. We didn't go to Florida with Mom, with Karen," I tried explaining in a way he'd understand.

"Oh, okay," he said back. It was a phrase he said often. I wasn't sure if he was truly understanding or that it was something he had learned to do to feign understanding.

"What about you guys? Did you two have fun this weekend?" I asked him, hoping to elicit something of substance from his past several days of being watched by several of our close family members.

"Oh, it was good. We laughed and giggled."

I had heard that phrase quite often from him, too. It was one of his stock answers when he couldn't remember specifics in response to a question. On one hand, I was happy he had a good time living with us, but simultaneously, it broke my heart to hear him say that. It was like a voice trying to call out from under a fog of memory loss.

Our trip to Florida had been a stark contrast. We'd had hours of deep conversation with my birth family. It felt good to talk on such an in-depth level, something that was missing with Dad. I had grown accustomed to the surface-level, repetitive conversations that are a signature of advancing dementia. Coming back home and talking with Dad brought home the harsh reality of the toll the disease takes on loved ones.

※

The next morning I would go back to my old routine, mixed with several new routines. Before sunrise, I'd make my slow walk downstairs, letting Angie sleep in. I'd make my coffee and read the news on my iPad. Then I'd get the daily newspaper at our front door and drop it off at the foot of Dad's back door as I walked to my car.

Now, on my half-hour drive to work, I'd often make a phone call to my grandfather, Grampy, who lived with Auntie Laura. He was an early riser as well and we'd enjoy a good chat during my commute. This was a great new addition to my routine.

My day at work and my evenings would mostly be the same, except for the daily texting and talking with Christina. I'd also get a group chat hello from my mom to both sisters and me, almost every morning. These were amazing additions to my life. They were rays of light that balanced my daily reminders from Dad that dementia robs a person from your life.

I would see changes in his functioning whenever I spent time with him. But whatever dementia took from him, it hadn't stolen his entire routine yet. The Monday night after we returned from Florida was his bowling night. When I came into his room, his bowling ball bag was sitting next to the door, as he sat on the couch waiting for me to come over to say it was time to go. Once again, he was wearing the same shirt he had been wearing from the weekend. It was stained on the sleeve.

"Dad," I said almost instinctively. I wanted him to look presentable to his bowling buddies, but it would be the same conversation we'd had so many times and I knew the drill. It would almost inevitably lead to a full blown shouting match, most likely ruining both our evenings.

"Hello. Is it time to go?" he asked.

Instead, I paused. He didn't know yet that I was about to call attention to his stained shirt. But I knew something. I knew that once I did that, he would get defensive and we'd soon be arguing. So, I continued to not say anything.

During this extended moment of silence, I had a flash back to the moment Sarah and I were at the beach and I so eagerly wanted to get into the water. At that instant, she too had paused. Her face had hesitated for just a split second. Instead of saying no, she just let it go. She stood up and joined me in the water. She did that for my sake.

My hesitation with replying to Dad was enough of a pause that I was able to change my mind about with what to say. Instead of insisting on being right and pointing out his failing due to his dementia, I hesitated, then let it go, for his sake.

I tried a different tactic.

"Hey Dad, didn't Angie just get you a nice dark gray sweater? I think it's right over here. I bet she'd love to see how good you look in it. Let's try that on quickly, if you don't mind. You'd be the hit at the bowling alley too, all snazzy like that."

"Okay."

Okay? He said yes? No argument. Instead of pointing out his flaw, I had redirected his focus to the new sweater. It worked. We changed his shirt to the clean one and not one argument ensued.

It was an amazing change from our standard interactions. All because I had reconsidered my motives. Instead of focusing on my being right, I took the back seat and focused on his well being. Like Sarah had done, I allowed myself to not be driven by my own selfishness, but placed the other person first. We had only known each other briefly so far, but my younger sister was already teaching me lessons, even from a thousand miles away.

God has a way of speaking to us through scripture in multiple ways and being a catalyst for change. Paul's letter to the Philippians is one example that spoke strongly to me. My translation, while it does not have the best English flow, follows more closely to the grammatical structure and thinking of the Greek text:

> *"Do not one thing according to selfish ambition or empty conceit, but in humility, considering one another as being better than oneself. Look out not only for the things of yourselves, but also the things of every one else." (Philippians 2:3-4, personally translated from the Byzantine Greek Text)*

I had read this many times and never really gotten it. But today, this verse spoke to me loud and clear.

And as I reflected on this, Dad and I had an evening filled with more fun than ever before. I allowed him to have the enjoyment he should have been having. I was glad that he was happy. But dementia is a horrible disease that changes a person and, really, steals them away from their loved ones in a slow and sad way.

As his mental state deteriorated slowly, I couldn't help but wonder more about my biological dad. How was his health? Was he still alive? Who was he? Would meeting him be similar to meeting my mom? He was about ten years older than my mom. If I were to find him, it had to be soon.

Ciao, Mi Chiamo Scott

"Ciao, mi chiamo Scott," began the first of a series of messages I sent. After the Florida trip, I knew so much more about my biological father. I could finally begin a real search for him. I now knew his name, Pietro, for the first time in my life. I was determined to find him.

However, I also had several obstacles that would require me to work significantly harder than my last search. The largest one was language. Additionally, I had to deal with the geographic distance and a six-hour shift in time zone; a different culture that was significantly more private than American culture; and I had no Italian Bad Bob to help me narrow down my search to those who were genetically linked to me.

The first decision I made was to submit my DNA to more companies. If I cast the net wider, perhaps I would find a European connection. There were some Italians in the results, but most were so distant that it wouldn't help. Strike one.

"He lives in northern Italy," my mother had told me during our trip. "I think it was in the San Pellegrino area. It had something to do with their water being very good."

I didn't know much about Italy, so I did some digging. San Pellegrino Terme is in the northern part of Italy in a region called Lombardy, and it's where we get the famous bottled water with the same name. It was a good start, I thought.

Also, it was only an hour and a half northeast from both Milan and Lake Como.

As I sat in our kitchen with Angie looking at the map, I said to her, "Look how close San Pellegrino is from Milan. We were so close." Just two years earlier we had been walking the streets of Milan.

※

In the middle of March, 2016, Angie and I had travelled to Italy together. She had been hired to draw for a company that was holding a conference at a beautiful resort on the coast of Lake Como. So we made it into a little vacation and extended our stay so we could explore Como and Milan together.

It was the first time I had been to a non-English-speaking country. We vacationed in Ireland in 2014, but it's much easier to get around when you speak the language.

So, on the plane flight we tried to memorize a few Italian phrases. "Dov'è il bagno?" "Il conto, per favore." "Vorrei un vino rosso." And of course the ever popular "Buon giorno" and "Grazie." We could ask for directions to the bathroom, ask for the check, and say thanks. We were set.

Despite our thick American accents, and that we didn't roll our *r* sounds, we got by okay since most everyone recognized instantly that our Italian was horrible and they smiled and dropped into English for our benefit. The advantage of staying in a tourist location.

Walking around the plaza in front of the cathedral Duomo di Milano is an experience that I will never forget. It is like stepping into a movie. The pigeons flock around the large open plaza waiting for food to fall from passing tourists. Duomo di Milano - the largest church in Italy - towers over the plaza. Countless spires spread across the multiple towers reached up into the sky as we sat looking at its gothic architecture.

After taking a few photographs for a travel book I was going to make of our trip, we strolled alongside the edge of the neighboring buildings and storefronts as vendors hawked everything from scarves to cheap Italian flag refrigerator magnets. Food vendors were everywhere, and we lit up when we saw one selling roasted chestnuts.

Milan in March is still chilly enough that we needed jackets, but comfortable enough to take a leisurely stroll along the plaza. Roasted chestnuts were a welcome find for nibbling in that brisk air.

As we walked away from the cathedral and down *via dei Mercanti*, a wide pedestrian only street, we both were getting a bit hungry and stopped at an outdoor restaurant out on the street. They had about twenty tables setup on the street with space heaters warming the tables under a large white tent.

Drinking a cappuccino and watching people strolling by, Angie and I began dreaming about moving to Italy.

"It really is amazing here. I am loving it," I told her. She agreed.

"I know. Remember when you wanted to move to Ireland? This is so much better."

"Yeah. I know." Years ago, I did want to move to Ireland. Until we actually visited it. While I loved that country, I realized pretty quickly during our trip that Ireland was not a country I would want to live in. It was beautiful, but just not a place I could call home. Italy was different. There was just something about it in Italy that we both fell in love with.

What was it that made me love it here? I wondered as I sat there. I was completely at home, despite not speaking the language or even having seen the rest of the country.

※

It would take two years before I learned that the source of my affection might be in my DNA; that my father, and his father before him, had roots deep in this northern Italian soil. When I learned just how Italian I was, and that my father might indeed still be living here, Angie and I found ourselves staring at the map of Italy in our kitchen one day in August 2018.

"Should we fly back to Milan and visit San Pellegrino?" Angie asked. She knew how much I wanted to find my father and now we had a pretty good idea where to search for him.

"I'd love to. Maybe we do some searching first, and by the time we go back in October, we might even have more information to find him."

Earlier that year, we had booked a return trip to Italy in October, 2018, this time with my brother and his wife. I only saw my brother one or two times a year since he had moved several states away after college, got married, and settled down.

I thought this would be a good opportunity to spend some time with him. We'd travel together to both Rome and Florence in a rented car.

"If we find your father, maybe we could drive up to meet him," I said to Angie.

Meet him? Just the thought was incredible, especially after my recent Florida trip. I now had a deadline. I had to find my father by October, just two months away.

This time we had a little more of an advantage. Near the end of 2017, both Angie and I had started taking private Italian lessons. We knew for sure we wanted to move to Italy. Angie was also mostly Italian. For the first few months, I thought the lessons were fun, but I was still taking my Greek lessons as well, so my Italian suffered.

By the beginning of 2018, when I received my DNA results and learned about my Italian heritage, I doubled down on learning the language. I ended Greek lessons so I could spend more time learning Italian, but I was still a far cry from being fluent.

So when I began searching for my father, I cheated a little and used Google Translate to help compose the initial messages I sent out asking about him. After all, October was quickly approaching, and I wanted to cast as wide a net as possible. Using machine translation with an online tool probably made me sound even worse at Italian.

To make things worse, Pietro is the Italian version of Peter and is a very popular name in Italy. That his name was common, that my initial messages were horrible, and that Italians in the north have a private nature probably all contributed to my getting many non-answers to my messages. They simply never replied back.

I thought back to Christina and her search for me and hearing "no" so often. She'd also had a large number of people not respond. I now felt the pain she had experienced. Not hearing back was almost worse than hearing a denial. For every twenty messages I sent, I might have heard back from only one or two.

It was looking as though I wasn't going to find him by October.

※

Sure enough, October came without any word of my father. The four of us flew to Rome, landing in Italy early in the morning after a long, overnight flight from JFK Airport. Catching a red eye flight out of New York City to Rome was longer than I had figured. Last time, it didn't seem as long. My first assumption was that I would sleep the whole night. Silly me.

Once in Italy, that didn't matter. It was great to be back. Especially because now, even though I hadn't found him, I knew he was here somewhere.

I was physically closer to him here. I was now in his country. *My country.* As I drove out of the airport rental car garage, this knowledge that my father lived here right now, made me feel more at home in Italy. While I should have been dead tired from lack of sleep, I wanted to soak in as much of Italy as I could.

I drove north to Florence along E35, the main highway that connects Rome to the north. It's a well-travelled route through the Italian countryside. Similar to Lancaster, there were farms for much of the drive, dotted with countless small towns along the rolling hills. In the distance, off to the right, we saw a series of large mountains running along the highway. It reminded me of the Appalachian mountains back home. But much higher.

Stunning, I thought. *Yeah, I could live here.*

We began talking about the half-marathon as we drove through Tuscany. Inside the Tuscan region is the Chianti area, well known for its red wines. Several weeks before our trip, my brother's wife had discovered that there was a half-marathon happening in Chianti. It was a trail run that literally weaved through the vineyards and alongside the castles of the Chianti countryside. We were all avid runners, but she was especially dedicated, having run several full marathons. In fact, she was well on her way to running a marathon in each state. Running a race in Italy sounded too good to pass up.

Friday was our first day in Florence. We walked along the river that winds its way through the city, and saw the statue of David. As evening approached, I guided our small group up the southern hill that climbs up to the Piazzale Michelangelo. A friend who had recently been to Florence told me how you could catch an incredible view of the city from this plaza.

As the sun dipped to the horizon, it cast a golden glow onto the red-tiled dome of the Cathedral of Santa Maria del Fiore, built in the 1200s. I spent about half an hour on the overlook of the plaza taking pictures during that 'golden hour' of sunset so treasured by photographers.

It was a fantastic and leisurely day in this historic city. The next two days would be farther south in the countryside for Chianti Classico Marathon. Saturday we spent registering for the half-marathon while others registered for the full marathon.

And we ate. How could we not enjoy more fine Italian dining? We ate at a fireside restaurant at our resort on a mountainside, overlooking the vast rolling hills to the west, and went to bed early, ready for Sunday morning and the race itself.

This was my first half-marathon, and I was doing it in Italy. How appropriate, I thought.

As I ran through the vineyards, I thought about my father. He was here, not too much farther north, most likely. I wish we had found him so we could be spending time with him on this trip.

So close, I kept thinking.

On Monday, we drove south towards Rome. We would then take a train from Rome even farther south, past Naples to Pompeii, and hike Mount Vesuvius. I was looking forward to it, but as we drove south, I felt like I was driving away from my father.

In that moment, it felt like I was losing two fathers at the same time. The first to dementia, the second to time. I knew my adoptive dad was on a steady decline, and it was hard knowing I would never have any deep talks with him. Driving south felt like leaving my biological father behind, even though I had not even found him. He was like a ghost that kept eluding me.

On our last night in Italy, I prayed that once I returned stateside and resumed reaching out to possible connections, we would find him. God's timing was perfect for me to find the first half of my family in Boston and Florida. I knew I could trust him to have worked out my search for my father.

Adopting Ideas

This busy year was also the year of my high school's 25th class reunion, which was being held four miles from my house. Many friends had been following my search and recent trip to Florida on social media and were looking forward to the reunion to hear more about my story of meeting my family.

That Saturday, my wife and I drove through the hilly countryside and pulled up on Front Street, just across the train tracks from the Susquehanna River and a block down from the restaurant hosting the reunion. We went inside, and thus began a whirlwind evening, catching up with friends. About halfway through, I finally was able to say hello to a friend with whom I had recently reconnected online. Samantha and I had been talking quite a bit on social media about my adoption and my search for my biological family, and all the emotions that came with it. She was eager to talk with me in person.

We grabbed a table nearby, out on the restaurant's back patio. Over the muffled sound of music from the '80s and '90s playing inside, she began to ask me about it. Samantha was especially interested because she and her husband had adopted a beautiful little girl several years ago.

"So, were you overwhelmed?" she asked. Angie sat next to me at the table and listened with Sam as I answered.

"Not as much as I thought I'd be." I said, as I began to chronicle the entire story, along with the emotions I had experienced during these past few weeks. I also began to articulate out loud, for the first time, some of the thoughts I had been meditating on recently, the most prominent being the idea of adoption in a broader sense.

"I'm blown away by how God describes heavenly things by using ideas that we can relate to. Like adoption. God adopted me. My mom also adopted me. I did nothing to earn God's love. I also didn't do anything to earn my mom's love. They both brought me into their family out of sheer love. They also made huge sacrifices in order for me to be adopted into their families," I began telling Sam.

"I know," she replied. She was also a strong believer and fully understood God's use of adoption to bring us into his family through Christ's sacrifice on the cross. "It's like we don't deserve to belong to his family, but by his action, we do belong to him."

There was that word again. *Belong.*

"Yes! I love how you said that," I said, almost cutting her off. "That sense of belonging. It's something I've been thinking about a lot recently. My whole life, I felt like I was different from everyone else. My mom adopted me and gave me everything. I felt so loved. But somehow, deep down, I knew I didn't do anything to deserve it. On one hand, it made me feel special that she went out of her way to bring me into her family. But on the other hand, for years, I felt like I was missing that sense of belonging.

"These past several months of searching and finally these past few weeks of meeting my biological family, I found out that I did belong. I now could see, through them, the same thing I saw in my wife, and the same thing my adoptive family had given me, despite my being too insecure and afraid to notice it.

"All of them had shown me unconditional love," I told her. "They had shown me grace beyond anything I deserved. They were extending a hand to create an unbreakable bond with me. But, until now, I never saw it."

Earlier that week, during the moment with Dad, was when it had all connected for me. Humility. Placing others before myself. That's what I had been missing, not an unbreakable bond. The bond had been offered to me all along.

I thought back to my time as a kid with my family at the beach in New Jersey. They had been the normal ones this whole time. I was the one who was wrong. The reason they were able to hold normal conversations and bond with each other was because they were able to overlook each other's faults. I was the only one focusing on the faults, and because of that, I was unable to let my guard down and simply enjoy their company. My life had been one constant act, pretending I was someone I was not. All this time, just as God passed over my faults, my family had been overlooking my arrogance and every other one of my faults.

By focusing on the faults of others, I was not able to accept that those faults would be forgiven. I was forgetting the work of the gospel in me, what God had done for me. I saw myself as better than them. This arrogance in my thinking had, my entire life, been placing myself above everyone else. Humility had left me in exchange for empty conceit, the very thing Paul had warned against.

I had distorted the gospel to believe my wrongs were forgiven because I was more worthy and God loved me more than others. But that's not the gospel message. And by viewing others this way, defining them by their faults, I was showing my own distrust of God's ability to cleanse them and forgive them. I was doubting the power of the gospel.

The reason I was able to get along so well with my wife was simply that I had let my guard down with her. She had done it first. She was completely open with me. My own family had been open and loving with me, too, except that for some reason I had been too afraid to return that love within my family. That I was able to do so with Angie allowed our bond to grow. And despite every bit of analytical and observational skill I had at my disposal, I was too blind to see what that meant.

It wasn't until I saw this unconditional love shown to me by my biological family that I finally was hit over the head with a wooden post. I was letting my guard down with them as I had done with Angie. I had been so distracted by the fun I was having with them that I was overlooking any faults and just being me.

I was beginning to understand what I was really seeking. I'd thought at first that the object was an unbreakable bond with someone. I thought I was searching for someone who got me. But during the journey I began to discover that I was looking in the wrong direction. Instead of looking for someone out there who was like me, I needed to look inward. I began *searching for me.*

※

"That unbreakable bond was there all along," I told Samantha. "I felt like Dorothy being told by the Wizard that I had these traits all along. My own insecurities made me direct attention away from me and towards the faults of others. I became more vocal at pointing out others' faults to better direct attention away from mine."

Once I understood that, and was able to focus on the interests of others instead of myself, I was able to admit my faults, like my pride. It is still difficult for me. But I am getting better at overcoming my arrogance and admit those faults.

"Before meeting my biological family," I told Samantha, "I felt that emptiness more than ever before. That became a driving factor for me to go on an ultimate search for someone like me. Amazingly, I found them. But it wasn't until I put the pieces of the puzzle together that I realized that the unbreakable bond I found with them wasn't simply because they were like me but because, in building our friendship, I simply let my guard down. I wasn't looking for faults anymore."

When Christ came to earth and dwelt with us - as scripture says, "pitched his tent among us" - he perfectly showed us the ultimate example of humility, I said to Samantha. He was God entering into his own creation as one of us, so that he could wipe away all the faults and ugly desires that we hold onto so tightly. He gives us a new heart, one that lets us desire him more than our own self-interest. It's a beautiful gift we don't deserve but is given to us anyway.

Samantha looked at me, thinking about it all. I was so focused on our conversation that I no longer heard the music in the background.

"It is exactly like adoption," she said. "You were adopted and given a new family. You didn't do anything to earn it. It was given to you. You were brought into a new, loving family, just as Christ came to earth to suffer for us and die for us. He did it so we didn't end up with eternal punishment, and second, and more importantly, he did it so we could be with him for eternity. He adopted us into his family. He built an unbreakable bond with us, just like you were given these incredible bonds with both of your families."

She was right.

※

And while I still fail often at it, this is how I try to see everyone now. I want to adopt them into my family. Treat everyone I meet as if they were my brother or sister. Love them unconditionally and open my heart to them. It's a stark contrast to what I was before. And I'm still far from doing this as often as I should. I still have those ugly thoughts more often than I like.

One thing I found myself doing more frequently was confessing my wrongs and keeping them at the front of my mind so I could ask God to forgive me. It's a powerful reminder, too, of my imperfections and broken nature and allows me to be forgiving of others and welcome them into my life with true love.

I'm far from perfect. I don't spread the word of God as often as I should. But I'm trying. And the more I do, the more connections I build with people. And the deeper those connections are.

In reality, we are all connected. We really don't have to go looking for those unbreakable bonds. They are there, ready to be uncovered. Understanding this has allowed me to find some incredible and unbreakable bonds with others, like my siblings.

Adoption is a beautiful thing. It is unconditional love.

When parents bring an adopted son or daughter into their lives, they promise to treat that child as one of their own for life. They are saying they will love that boy or girl more than anything else in their lives. Like my mom did for me throughout my life. Like Angie did. Like my biological family did.

Adoption is a sign of the incredible love a parent has for a child. That unbreakable bond was there for me from the very beginning, despite my failure to recognize it.

We are not alone. We are adopted into one giant family of God through the work of Jesus Christ. You are loved by him. Trust in the work that he has done for you and allow him to adopt you, as I was.

I was born. I was adopted. I went searching for me. I found a sense of belonging and an unbreakable bond.

※

"To all who received him, namely the ones believing in the name of him, he gave to them the right to be born children of God, who were born, not from bloodlines, nor out of the will of flesh, nor out of the will of man, but from God." (John 1:12-13, personally translated from the Byzantine Greek Text)

※

Epilogue

It was becoming a normal part of my routine. "Ciao, mi chiamo Scott," I would write to countless Italians each week. "Hi, my name is Scott."

Almost all ignored my message.

Christina was the perfect sibling to support me in this search. She of all people understood what I was going through in looking for my biological father. She literally had done the same for years searching for me. She let me know she understood the struggle as I continued to push forward in this search.

By early 2019, I had started to feel numb to the replies from my messages, each basically saying, "No. Sorry but the person I know by that name does not match your description." I had added what I knew about my father: his name, the ship name and years on which he worked on it. But months of searching had turned up no one who knew him.

Then, on February 28, 2019, I received another response from one of the messages I sent out.

"Ciao. Si, Pietro è mio papa."

Hello. Yes, Pietro is my father.

Thanks

Thank you for reading *Searching For Me*.

I very much hope you enjoyed reading my book, and that you might be inspired to write a brief review of it. Those reviews help me enormously.

Lastly, I'd love to have you as a subscriber to my readers' newsletter. For an exclusive bonus chapter of this book, plus previews of new books and more, sign up:

SullysBrain.com/news-searching

Made in the USA
Middletown, DE
16 January 2020

83323857R20116